NFT – INCOME FOR CREATIVE MINDS

HOW TO GENERATE ADDITIONAL INCOME AS A PHOTOGRAPHER, GRAPHIC DESIGNER, COMPOSER, MUSICIAN OR OTHER ART CREATOR

PIO X. PERDUTO

Copyright © Pio X. Perduto
All Rights Reserved.

Contents

Foreword

At the latest since there have been press reports that digital artworks have been sold for millions in leading auction houses around the world, some artists may have wondered whether this could be a source of income for them. Some have already jumped on the bandwagon and in some cases have generated considerable income, while others have - apparently - done the same, but possibly lost money as well as time.

I myself, also a creator of art, asked myself the same question. I, too, was initially put off by the many cryptic terms such as blockchain, hashing, cryptocurrency, Ethereum, non-fungible tokens, and so on. But at some point, my curiosity got the better of me and I got to grips with the terms. In the process, I learned on the one hand what was behind all these strange terms, and on the other hand, I also offered and already sold my own digital artworks online. Admittedly, the millions are still a long time coming! Nevertheless: For the beginning I am enormously satisfied and happy about income from sales as well as those from resales by my buyers (if you can't imagine that yet, don't worry about it, we will discuss it in detail in the course of this book).

However, I realized relatively quickly that it's not enough to simply create interesting works and put them somewhere on the Internet. Thousands of people around the world are doing this, and standing out from the crowd and generating sales is about as likely as placing a daily classified ad in any newspaper that people can buy art from you. You might actually find a potential buyer this way. However, it would probably be a matter of chance.

So if you want to become successful with NFT and generate recurring income from your art, there are some further measures to take. There are many ways to do this and some of them lead to the goal more easily, others more difficult or with greater detours and a lot of effort. I have already made these experiences and in this book I would like to offer you a shortcut, so to speak. Instead of listing all the mistakes - some of which I have made myself and some of which have also cost me a lot of money and time - I would like to offer you a shortcut.

I offer you the opportunity to benefit from my experience and to start from the pole position.

I wish you much success with your art and its marketing, and I hope that with the help of the insights and information in this book you will be able to create a solid additional income that will allow you to continue to devote yourself to your art. The information in this book is valuable - in any case, too valuable to be read and forgotten. The book can help you market your art. But this presupposes that you become active and take action!

The Author

Acknowledgements

In this book you will also find screenshots of websites. These are of course to be understood as a quotation and not my work. The source results from the context. It may be that screenshots will change over time.

The prices quoted in the book can fluctuate greatly depending on price developments, demand, adjustments to price lists, etc. In any case, it is recommended to verify the current prices before listing and selling NTFs in order to be able to design offers in such a way that they also lead to actual income and do not only cause costs.

CHAPTER ONE

What are NFTs?

When we talk about NFTs, we should first be clear about what NFTs, Non Fungible Tokens, are. I would like to address this in the following subchapters:

ax. What is an NFT?
ax. Why are NFTs valuable?
ax. What are blockchain and blockchain protocols?
ax. The main types of NFTs

Caution: This is not a book for technicians or people who want to understand the technology behind NFT in detail. There are other publications for that. Within the scope of this text, we only want to deal with the technical basics to the extent that we understand the interrelationships that we need in order to be successful with NFT.

What is an NFT?

If we want to understand NFTs, we should first briefly look at the evolution of the Internet.

Web 1.0

In the beginning, in the 1990s, the Internet was a platform that people accessed to get information. Most people couldn't really publish their own content, or if they could, it was only at an extremely rudimentary level. In order to design a website, people had to have certain technical skills. It was necessary to know HTML and, for applications that went beyond displaying fixed text, more advanced programming languages. This excluded a large proportion of people from publishing their own content. They used the Internet accordingly to consume content provided by others - often by companies and organizations.

Web 2.0

In the 2000s, the Internet continued to develop This was, of course, possible to a large extent because the number of users increased steadily, which meant that much more money flowed into developments. Also, more and more people actively engaged with the Internet and the underlying mechanisms and techniques. During this time, platforms like Twitter, Facebook, Instagram, etc. became big. Users were now no longer just consumers. They were able to easily upload their own content such as text, images, graphics, videos, sound files, etc. to the Internet and make it accessible to a worldwide audience. To do this, they no longer needed in-depth technical understanding or special technical skills. The camera in a cell phone can be used to take pictures and videos, which can then be edited as desired using apps, some of which are available free of charge, and finally uploaded to various platforms.

Departure into Web 3.0

Now, in the 2020s, there will be another quantum leap in the technology and application of the Internet, and this is to a large extent related to a technology that we will look at in more detail a little later: blockchain technology. In this context, users of the Internet are increasingly also becoming co-owners and co-operators. We are only at the beginning of this development, but it can already be seen today that this is a quantum leap in development, which will lead to us as Internet users being excluded from any large operators will become increasingly independent. Cryptocurrencies, NFTs, smart contracting, and many more are just the beginning of what this technology can produce in the coming years.

Attempt to define NFTs

If you are looking into the topic of NFT, there is a good chance that you have at least a basic understanding of what an NFT or Non Fungible Token is. That said, let's address the question briefly to make sure we're all talking about the same issue.

As a person who creates art, you are probably familiar with this situation: you have created a work - whether it is a visual work, an acoustic work, or a work that appeals to one or more (other) senses. For simplicity's sake, let's assume it's a visual work, such as an oil painting. You could create a second painting on the same subject, but it would never be a 100% copy.

Differences in color application, brush strokes, etc. might not be perceptible at first glance, but they would be upon closer analysis. Of course, you could also photograph the picture and pass it on as a photograph or print, and you could even scan it and have a painting robot make thousands of copies. Nevertheless, there would really only be one original. If, on the other hand, you had created a print, you might make a certain number of prints, which you number and sign. Thus there is a manageable number of originals.

However, one can now ask why what we perceive as an original is much more valuable than, for example, a copy or even a print. Are we less pleased with the colors, the expression, the picture's message? How can it be that a painting by Vincent van Gogh has a value in the millions just because he painted it himself, while an art print with exactly the same dimensions and colors can be had for the cost of a dinner? If you look at both paintings with a little distance, you may not even be able to tell the difference.

The difference in value has not so much to do with the picture's message, but rather with its rarity, which is recorded by signatures, certificates and proofs of ownership. There is only one original painting, but potentially millions of reproductions. These certificates, which are supposed to ensure that a painting is indeed a work by Vincent van Gogh - and that it was not, for example, created by a talented forger - provide the buyer with proof of value, which makes it easier for him to resell the work, if that is what he is aiming for. On the other hand, this also leads to the buyer being the proud owner of a genuine, unique van Gogh painting.

NFTs also include certificates that uniquely identify digital objects and thus ensure that they cannot be falsified, copied or imitated. It goes without saying that a digital image can be copied an infinite number of times. However, the results of the copying process are always copies and there remains exactly one original whose status can be verified at any time by the NFT.

NFT technology is based on blockchain technology. Early forms of it can be traced back a long time. An early version of blockchain-like technology was described by David Chaum as early as 1982. "Bitcoins," probably the most blockchain-related application of this technology today, show 2008 as the year of birth. However, the technologies needed to implement NFTs can be traced back to the development of the ERC-721 standard, which was published in 2017. This standard made it possible to work with token-based smart contracts, which made it possible to create and process NFTs.

To understand NFTs, we should know what is meant by "non fungible." "Fungible" means exchangeable. A typical example of a fungible store of value is, for example, a ten-euro banknote. It is interchangeable. If I give my counterpart a banknote of ten euros and he gives me another one, we may have different papers before the transaction, but we both still have the same asset. Even if he gave me back two banknotes for five euros instead of a ten-euro banknote, neither he nor I would have the impression that we had lost anything as a result of this exchange.

Non-fungible plants are different. They are different from one another and no two are the same. Unlike the banknote example, an exchange would also be possible here, but it would first have to be agreed how the non-fungible (NF) assets involved would be valued. Would the value of NF1 and the value of NF2 be the same, so that the two owners could simply exchange them, so to speak, or would the owner of NF2 possibly have to add something to create equality of value?

Let us consider a real-life example. You may own an oil painting that has been in your family for many generations, and even if it wasn't painted by Vincent van Gogh, it still has a four-figure value. On the other hand, I recently found a drawing from my childhood in a shoe box. Like your painting, mine is a one-of-a-kind piece and was also created with a great deal of love and enthusiasm. Nevertheless, you probably would not consider an exchange of your painting for mine to be fair. The two paintings are therefore non-fungible in our perception.

Another important difference between fungible and non-fungible assets is that fungible assets can often be subdivided. Instead of the ten-euro banknote, you could also take ten individual euro coins, because the respective purchasing power is equivalent. This is also not feasible with our paintings.

One could name as properties of NFTs:

ax. They are unique at the cryptographic level and cannot be copied or replicated

ax.   NFT assets are created in the blockchain in the form of tokens
ax.   They are based on smart contracts[1]
ax.   They typically use the Ethereum ERC-721 or ERC-1155 standard

Why are NFTs valuable?

The question of what is valuable and why some things are considered valuable is almost a philosophical question. Why are people willing to work for days and exchange a wide variety of goods such as food, luxury goods and much more for paper - which, when lit, burns within seconds and barely gives off enough heat to warm even a thimbleful of coffee?

We are used to judging certain things as valuable and others not. Most people would consider a gold bar to be extremely valuable. But if I were traveling through the deserts of Africa and had nothing but a backpack full of gold bars and didn't meet a single person, I would probably be willing to trade all my gold for a single bottle of water in no time. There are many comparable examples. The basic message remains the same: value is hardly something absolute, but is made by people. A few years ago, the first generation iPhone was something that made people spend the night outside stores to be one of the first to own one of the coveted devices. Just two or three years later, people may have been ridiculed if they still owned this device. But soon collectors might be willing to pay a small fortune for a fully functional first-generation iPhone. That is the situation in our everyday world. But how does it behave in the digital world?

Values also exist in the digital world. Time and again, special Internet domains, which are actually just addresses on the Internet, i.e. have no physical equivalent, are sold or auctioned off for vast sums. Digital currencies such as Bitcoins, Ethereum and many others are acquired and traded by millions of people. The capitalization of Bitcoin alone - despite a massive drop in price in the last few months before I wrote this book - is still roughly equivalent to the gross national product of countries like Switzerland or Saudi Arabia. The next largest cryptocurrency, Ethereum, additionally brings it to about just under half of that.

In fact, most of the elements that exist in the normal world have equivalents in the digital world as well. Let's make a direct comparison:

In the "real world" (RW), ownership relationships are regulated by contracts, which are notarized by notaries or similar authorities when they reach a certain significance. In the "digital world" (DW), we work with smart contracts, which are use of blockchain technology are forgery-proof. This is the case with cryptocurrencies such as bitcoins, tokens and NFTs.

ax. In RW, the rarity of materials or items (gold, diamonds, artwork by famous artists, etc.) makes up the value. This is the same in DW, where rarity is guaranteed by tokens.

ax. In the RW, you can invest in companies and become a shareholder. In this way, you acquire a share in a company and benefit from its economic success and, depending on the structure, can also influence its development by exercising voting rights. In DW, the possibility of interaction and participation is found through the use and co-design of games and participation in DAOs[2] (Decentralized Autonomous Organizations), such as MutantCats (cf. Mutantcats.io) and comparable platforms and approaches.[3] and similar platforms and approaches. Here, participants can have a say in the investment strategy and thus actively shape the performance of their investment.

ax. In the real world, people with a certain amount of wealth can also do this within the framework of exclusive associations (country clubs, golf clubs, some business clubs, etc.) and exchange ideas in such a framework with people with similar interests and similar financial possibilities. Such clubs and organizations are also increasingly emerging in DW. One example is the Bored Ape Yacht Club[4] where people also purchase a membership and thus become members of an exclusive association.

ax. Status symbols such as special handbags, wristwatches and shoes or special car brands serve to a good extent to show a certain status. In this context, the possession of a certain product is supposed to convey a certain purchasing power and social status to other people.[5] In the DW, such status can be represented, among other things, by the possession of special NFTs. Those who buy a digital work of art for thousands or millions of euros often do so either as a financial investment or as a status object (often for both reasons). Presenting one's own collection within the framework of suitable platforms offers an opportunity for self-expression.

What are blockchain and blockchain protocols?

When we talk about the blockchain, this is not correct. In fact, there are lots of different blockchains, as the technology is used by a wide variety of organizations and providers. Probably the best known is the Bitcoin blockchain. However, there are also others such as those of Ethereum, WAX, Polygon, Solana, Tezos, Cardano or the Binance Smart Chain, to name just a few. Nevertheless, the market is dominated by a relatively small number of blockchains, with the Ethereum blockchain being the most widely used (but not the only one) in the context of NFTs. In addition, we will also come across the Polygon and Cardano blockchains in the further sections of the book, which are becoming increasingly important in the context of NFTs.

However, the number of users of a blockchain is a key factor for the marketing of products. It's as if we were to offer physical pictures in different stores, each of which only accepts the local currency. If the store is now located in the USA, we have a large, potential customer group, since even in the domestic market there are many millions of potential customers who, on the one hand, have money in USD and, on the other hand, probably also have the necessary purchasing power. However, if our store were now located in Iceland, for example, the restriction that the store only accepts local currency would mean that the number of potential buyers in the country would be one thousandth of the citizens of the USA. So the market would be much smaller. Comparably on the blockchain market, the Ethereum blockchain is the heavyweight and each of the other mentioned (and other) providers is only a lightweight. This is important because currently it is not possible to transfer an NFT from one blockchain to another. A disadvantage, on the other hand, is that the Ethereum blockchain in its current version[6] is rather slow and incurs high transaction costs.

But what actually is a blockchain? Let me try to express it as non-technically as possible. Imagine that you have a large amount of documents, which are not stored centrally, however, but of which a copy is held by all participants in the blockchain. Accordingly, unlike in a database-driven environment, there is not a certain entry in a field in the database that could be maliciously changed by one person, but rather the file with the entries exists on millions of computers. If data were now maliciously adjusted on one computer, this would have no effect, because purely based on the large number of the other computers in the network of computers would be overruled and the corresponding data would be identified as false. Manipulation would therefore have to take place on millions of computers in parallel, which is hardly feasible in itself.

Now there is a second technological feature that makes the information in the blockchain even more secure. Imagine that the data in the blockchain consisted of an infinite number of pages. In this case, the first thing that would always be displayed on a subsequent page would be the sum of the points[7] on the previous pages would always be displayed first on a subsequent page, and the corresponding number would of course in turn be included in the calculation of the sum of the subsequent page. If something were now adjusted on a page, the corresponding sum would no longer be correct and since the sum is also in turn included in the sums of all subsequent pages, any manipulation would be obvious. Thus, without the use of a central body, for example a register or notary, it can be ensured that the data contained is unchanged, and this can be traced by anyone at any time, since all transactions are completely transparent. Only the owners of the individual accounts need not be transparent. But then again, this means that ownership is tied to a corresponding account and not to a person. Whoever has access to the corresponding account[8], can fully dispose of the assets linked to it. On the other hand: If you should lose the access data to your account, you (and all others who do not have the access data either) no longer have the possibility to access it.

In particular, there is also no central authority that could simply create a new access for you (because they don't have access either). Don't worry too much about this, though. It is important to be careful, but this should apply to all activities on the Internet. However, there are measures and techniques that can help you protect your property.

The main types of NFTs

There are very different use cases and areas of application for NFTs. Let's look at a few examples together to give you an impression of the diversity. Perhaps one or the other will inspire you to also develop your own applications, which will work optimally with your art and your works:

ax. Physical and digital artworks - we will talk about this in a special way in the present book and go into further detail there ax. Collectibles: for example trading cards or digital collectibles like Bored Ape images[9]

ax. Media and sound files: The song The Source generated sales of USD 490 000 as NFT[10]

ax. Elements from video games

ax. Memes

ax. Game elements (e.g. from online games)

ax. Domain names

ax. Property in the real world

ax. u. v. a.

In principle, everything can be linked with NFTs. NFTs are actually only the certificates that clearly describe the ownership and which are unique due to the entry of the ownership in the blockchain. If ownership is sold, the NFT in the blockchain is transferred to another person, who is then the owner guaranteed by the blockchain. For example, it would be perfectly technically possible to hold entire land registers recording ownership of land, houses, apartments, etc., in a blockchain, eliminating the need for notaries and similar entities. The same is obviously true with regard to bank accounts - nothing else is being done in the context of the Bitcoin blockchain, for example - except that these are not "bank" accounts, of course, since no banks are required for this.

[1] We will look at this in more detail as the book progresses.

[2] from Wikipedia (accessed 1/2022): Decentralized autonomous organization (DAO), sometimes decentralized autonomous corporation (DAC), refers to an organization that is coded by a transparent computer program. The program is neither controlled by shareholders nor influenced by a central government. The financial transaction record and program rules of a DAO are maintained on a distributed ledger technology (DLT). The exact legal status of this type of business organization is unclear.

A well-known example of venture funding was The DAO, which launched in June 2016 with crowdfunding of $150 million and was immediately hacked of $50 million in cryptocurrency. This hack was reversed in the following weeks and the money was recovered via hard fork of the Ethereum blockchain. The decentralized rescue was made possible by a majority vote of the Ethereum community.

[3] Mutant Cats is the first DAO to purchase and fractionate Cool Cats, CryptoPunks, and more valuable blue chip NFTs for distribution to its

members.

The $FISH token represents fractions of Cool Cats held in the vault. Each Mutant Cat NFT earns 10 FISH per day through Staking.

In addition, each Mutant Cat NFT grants access to the exclusive DAO community and voting rights over DAO assets.

The Mutant Cat DAO provides holders with exclusive access to NFT drops, regularly claimable NFTs, and many other future utilities.

[4] https://boredapeyachtclub.com/#/home - we will come back to this club in the course of the book

[5] In doing so, it is usually generously overlooked that a large number of people who use or wear these things do not own them at all, but use them, if necessary, in the context of Borrow leases from the actual owner, a bank or leasing institution, or carry any copies of no value.

[6] a new version (Ethereum 2.0) is announced

[7] from which the letters are composed

[8] we will talk about the issue of account security at a later date

[9] have already been sold in some cases for millions

[10] https://www.youtube.com/watch?v=HNKf2X76NA0

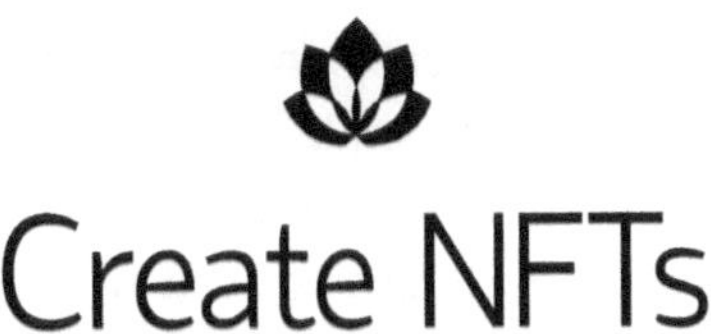

CHAPTER TWO

Create NFTs

There are dozens of marketplaces where NFTs can be offered and traded. Some are better known, others less so. Some allow anyone to be a vendor, others only allow people who have been invited or who have applied and been selected. New ones are added daily, and some - especially the smaller ones - may go away at some point. For this reason, I focus my explanation and presentation on the largest, most stable and most frequented platforms, as experience has shown that the risk of them suddenly closing their doors is lowest there. This does not mean, however, that once you have worked your way through the following topics, you should not look around for alternatives and, if necessary, find your own approaches.

Ethereum and other cryptocurrencies

Before we can start generating NFTs, we need money in a suitable currency. This is used to pay the gas fees for creating and trading NFTs. Conventional currencies such as euros, francs, dollars or yen cannot be used directly for this purpose, but must first be exchanged for the appropriate cryptocurrency. But what are cryptocurrencies actually?

The term cryptocurrency, also referred to as cryptocurrency or simply crypto, is derived from the ancient Greek κρύπτω krýpto (German 'verbergen', 'hide', 'schützen'). Alternatively used terms are also coins or tokens. They represent digital assets that are used as a medium of exchange (as is also the case with classic currencies). Unlike traditional money, there are no coins or banknotes, but the assets only exist digitally as an entry in the decentralized[1] database usually in a blockchain. The use of strong encryption algorithms ensures that transactions and their owners, as well as the creation and destruction of coins, can be secured and verified.

As of mid-2021, there were over 10,000 different cryptocurrencies in total, of which about 1% are also important internationally and beyond a narrowly defined community. In addition, there are also many cryptocurrencies that were created primarily to jump on the bandwagon during the Bitcoin hype and to pull money out of people's pockets. Therefore, before investing in any currency, it should always be checked whether a particular currency is also traded and held on a larger scale. Websites of crypto exchanges and dexes (decentralized exchanges) generally provide information on transaction volumes, price trends and capitalization.

In fact, it must be said that especially when investing in the less large and less widespread cryptocurrencies, a significant risk of loss is to be expected.

The digital version of a wallet or bank account is called a wallet. It is an address to which one's own funds can be transferred. These wallets can only be accessed with the help of a key. The owner of the key is considered the holder. This means that anyone who passes on this key is effectively handing over their assets to someone else. Anyone who loses or forgets the key will be faced with a closed door in the future if they want to access their assets. It is estimated that there are billions of forgotten or inaccessible assets that the original owner can no longer access.

One of the most widely used cryptocurrencies, which is also particularly important in the context of NFTs, is called Ethereum. Ethereum is an open-source distributed system that offers, among other things, the creation, management and execution of contracts in its own blockchain (this is also the basis for the use of NFTs). It uses its own cryptocurrency called Ether (abbreviated as ETH, symbol: Ξ) as a means of payment for transaction processing. After Bitcoin, Ether is the cryptocurrency that had the second largest market capitalization at the time this book was written and can thus be considered relatively stable.

It has become increasingly apparent in the past that Ethereum is relatively slow and cost- intensive. This is related to the algorithm currently still in use, which is based on a proof-of-work approach. This is to be replaced in the course of 2022 by a new version (Ethereum 2.0), which is based on a proof-of-stake algorithm[2] and is not only to be considerably faster, but also cheaper.

Cryptocurrencies can be purchased via a variety of apps and platforms. The number of corresponding platforms is constantly growing, and it is therefore advisable to take a close look at where you put your money. Forbes magazine published a helpful overview in January 2022 under the title "The Best Crypto Exchanges Of February 2022"[3]. The places 1: Coinbase, 2: Crypto.com and 3: Uphold differ significantly in terms of costs as well as in terms of the number of currencies traded. However, they can be considered stable and secure, just like the others ranked here. Unfortunately, this is not the case with all platforms.

To purchase cryptocurrencies, it is first necessary to open a corresponding account with a platform of one's choice and transfer money to it. Depending on the platform, this is done by paying with a credit or debit card and/or a bank transfer.

Some also offer other options such as instant bank transfer. It is important to check the corresponding options of the various providers. Most of them also have corresponding video explanations on their websites, which show the process of creating an account as well as the execution of corresponding transactions in detail. It is true that most providers are focused on the English-speaking world and offer their interfaces and services in English. However, an increasing number of providers now offer services for international users and enable use with screen interfaces and help pages in various other languages with wider, international distribution.

In order to be able to use the acquired cryptocurrencies for our NFT project, we now have to transfer them to a platform that we can use to carry out transactions with the marketplaces we use. In doing so, any fees incurred will be charged directly to the respective accounts and funds will be transferred directly to the platforms. This is also important because it means that you do not have to rely on the goodwill of any platform operators, but receive credits directly when they arise (for example, when your account is credited by the sale of NFTs). Again, there are a large number of such platforms, but the primary one recommended by Opensea.io (we'll talk about what that is later) is Metamask and accordingly we'll take a closer look at it.

Metamask.io sees itself as a gateway to a new dimension of the Internet 3.0, which aims to keep the data and assets of its users secure and easily available to the owner. Thus, it is possible to benefit from new services and platforms that do not regard the Internet user as a mere consumer and/or publisher, but rather give him the opportunity to help shape the Internet himself.

Metamask supports a wide range of currencies, platforms and technologies and, controlled by the user, enables data to be matched and logins to be used without any third-party providers owning this data and possibly being able to sell it on to third parties.

Conceivable activities, based on an Internet account with Metamask, are according to their own statement:

ax. Crowdfunding
ax. Choose
ax. Purchase of services and goods
ax. Offer and sell art

ax. Pay freelancers and get paid as a freelancer
ax. u. v. a.

Metamask offers users of the Chrome browser the advantage of having an official plugin that can be integrated into the Chrome browser. To do this, download the plugin and register for your own account during this process. In the process, during the identification process, you will also receive, among other things, a sentence with 12 simple words. This phrase is your access to the account in case you forget your password. It identifies you to Metamask as the owner. Keep this phrase safe and make sure you can find it at any time. Make sure that ONLY you can find it and not, for example, a technician when you bring your PC in for repair or an employee who cleans up your office, for example. The creation process is quite simple. Just try it. You will see that the process is done first class. You will notice that no one will ask you for an ID card or anything like that during this process. This is due to the fact that the account is not based on a government-verified identity, but manifests its own digital identity, which is represented by the possession of the account access. Even the operators of the platform do not know who is behind the individual accounts.

Then transfer the required cryptocurrency to your Metamask account. To do this, it is important that the account header says "Ethereum". This will address your Ethereum wallet. You can also trade multiple currencies in Metamask. In that case, you can switch between the different wallets by clicking the arrow and switching to the appropriate account.

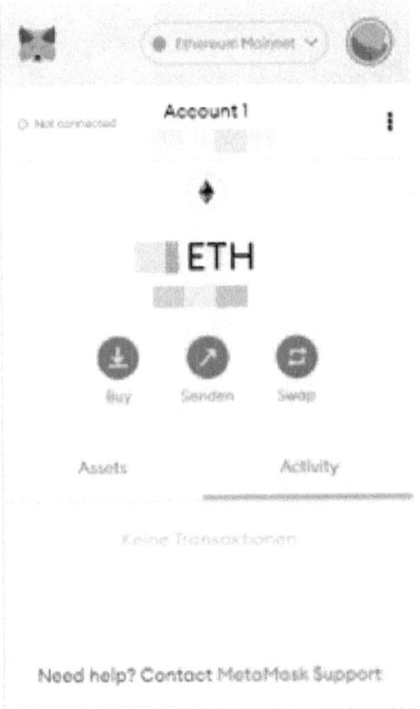

To transfer the already purchased Ethereum coins to Metamask now, go to "Buy" and select the last entry in the selection there:

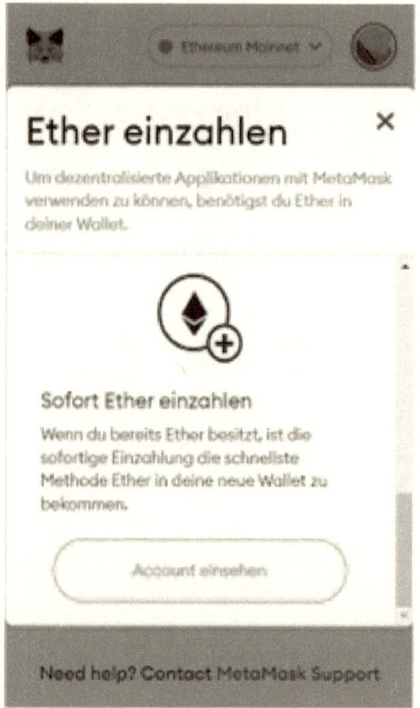

When you click on "View Account", a new page will be opened and a barcode will be displayed. You then scan this barcode with your cell phone in the app you used to buy the Ethereum coins.

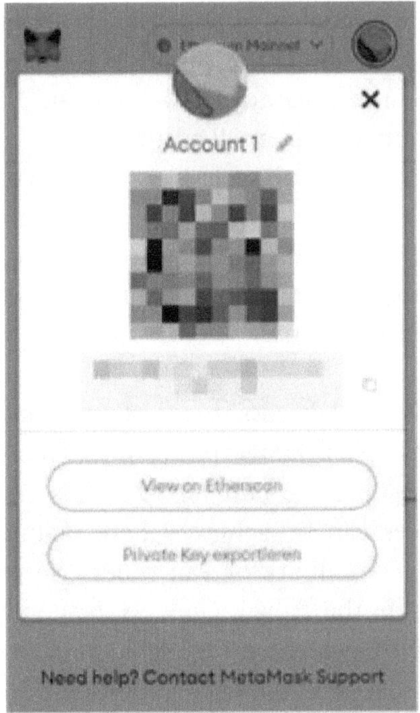

You can now still specify the amount you want to transfer to the account. The barcode corresponds to the corresponding account address. Normally, you will notice after a few minutes that the amount has been debited from the existing app and credited to your Metamask account. Attention: Each transaction costs fees, which consist of a basic fee and an amount-dependent fee. It is therefore advisable to transfer sufficient money at once, since a division into many small units would result in above-average transaction costs caused. We will address the issue of fees, which are incurred for every blockchain transaction, later.

NFT Marketplaces

As mentioned earlier, there are a lot of NFT marketplaces, i.e. marketplaces where NFTs are traded. Let's take a closer look at a few important ones. The choice of marketplace is important because an NFT that is posted on a marketplace will generally continue to be traded through that marketplace. Making the right choice can be critical. Some marketplaces are enormously large and also have high access numbers, which speaks for a high number of potential customers - but on the other hand also means that the number of suppliers is probably also enormously high. Accordingly, a large number of providers and NFTs compete for the interest and money of many potential customers.

On the other hand, there are relatively clear marketplaces where the number of suppliers is sometimes limited because suppliers can only sell via them after an assessment. These marketplaces often have fewer potential customers. Finally, there are topic-oriented marketplaces and those that only offer certain NFT products.

- ax. **Opensea.io** - We will discuss this platform in more detail afterwards. It is the largest NFT marketplace. It is true that the number of potential buyers and the number of sellers and NFTs on offer are very large. Sales can be achieved here mainly if the seller has a corresponding community or can otherwise promote his products to stand out from the crowd. One advantage of the platform is that only the first NFT posted on the platform incurs a gas fee when it is created. After that, any number of additional NFTs can be uploaded for free. This provides a certain filter against less serious providers, but makes the site attractive especially if the idea is to offer multiple NFTs.

- ax. **Rarible.com** - Also a very large marketplace site with a large audience and many sellers. Personally, I find the site more appealing than Opensea.io in its structure and features, but it's definitely worth just taking a look at both from the customer's point of view and see where your own works would fit better. To do this, analyze realized sales first and foremost. They are decisive - not the number of works offered.

- ax. **Foundation.app** - Is a slightly smaller platform. It has the advantage over Opensea.io and Rarible.com that the gas fees we have to invest to offer things are lower.[4] which we have to invest to offer things are lower. A nice feature is the LiveView function, which shows the current offers in real time, giving a good impression of activities and market. However, on this page, only someone who has been invited by an existing foundation provider can offer.

ax. **Mintable.app** - This platform is characterized from the provider side mainly by the fact that no gas fees are incurred for the posting of NFTs. This has the effect that there is a huge offer here and some providers offer their works for peanuts (a few euros) and thus the prices are quite "in the basement". Nevertheless, it can be useful to have a closer look at the platform.

ax. **Niftygateway.com** - Offers sellers the ability to offer NFTs without having a wallet (a wallet for cryptocurrencies) or any cryptocurrencies. In order to sell through this platform, it is necessary to apply. The application process includes, among other things, the need to show one's various social media accounts. This is to ensure that only sellers who also have enough sales potential and a sufficiently extensive community are on the website.

There are many other platforms besides the ones mentioned. In the following text, we will take a closer look at the three platforms Opensea, Rarible and Mintable, since anyone can offer their services there and no special requirements have to be met.

Gas-Fees

When someone wants to sell works on a NFT marketplace, in most cases fees, so-called gas fees, are incurred. While Opensea.io only charges a gas fee for the first NFT created, some other sites charge a gas fee for posting every single NFT. In addition, there is always a gas fee when a work is sold. This is generally deducted directly from the buyer's payment. Thus, if an NFT is to be posted in a marketplace that charges a gas fee for posting, it is necessary to have sufficient cryptocurrencies, in most cases Ether, in one's wallet before posting it[5].

The price of gas fees is not static, but varies depending on the traffic. The more people also want to carry out transactions via a platform at a given time, the higher the gas fee incurred. In other words, the more demand there is for the computing power available to perform the transactions, the more it costs. Experience has shown that gas fees tend to be cheapest in the early morning (European time zones), as many people in the USA are still asleep at this time and there is correspondingly less demand. From experience, the gas fees can be the equivalent of about 80 to 150 euros in Ether.

However, this will probably be corrected sharply downwards after the introduction of the new protocol - probably in the 2nd half of 2022. In any case, care should be taken to ensure that there is sufficient cover in the wallet to carry out the corresponding transactions.

Create a first NFT

Since I assume that you are already artistically active, your first NFT will probably be a work from your portfolio, or you may decide to develop your own works for the NFT theme. In either case, you should look to the various marketplaces for guidance in selecting what to offer. Find out what sells there and what may not be of interest. Personally, I am always surprised that some of my best works are hardly noticed by a large number of potential customers, while other works are met with enormous interest, even if I myself count them among my weaker ones.

Of course, you can ignore it completely and offer what you consider particularly successful. You might even find someone who shares your assessment and, with luck, an interested person might decide to invest money in your work. However, you must assume that people who invest in NFTs are also always thinking about what performance their investment is likely to have. People generally don't buy NFTs to hang up somewhere.

If you want to appeal to this type of customer, you might want to offer your art more as an art print or something similar[6]. NFTs are largely bought - at least in part - as an investment. In most cases, people who invest money in them will also look at where the demand is, so that positive performance is likely.

Although it probably goes without saying, if you want to create and sell NFTs, you must own the rights to the works you offer. This can be of particular importance if, for example, you work based on the works of other artists, for example, by processing image or sound files as part of your works - for example, by integrating parts of an image into one of your graphics or using a sound file in the soundtrack of a video. You can do both, as long as you have clarified the rights issue accordingly. In some cases, this requires that you acquire the corresponding rights, in other cases, the corresponding original artists simply want to be named. In any case, you should pay attention to the issue of copyright. After all, you will certainly also want people to respect your copyrights. In addition, copyright infringements are also - rightly - pursued more and more intensively and corresponding violations can quickly lead to high costs.

Now, how you turn your work into NFTs is something we'll look at in more detail as part of the presentation of the different platforms.

Rarible.com

Let's start with Rarible.com. You undoubtedly have the most important thing by now: Your work, which you would like to sell as NFT. If you don't have one yet, and maybe you're not even artistically active, you can find thousands of ways and possibilities to create suitable works. Of course, you can also be inspired by what other artists do and what is successful. Of course, you should not make copies of the works of other artists, but to be inspired by the works of others is common practice and part of the development of many great artists of world fame.

Now, if you want to create an NFT on Rarible, just go to the "Create" button that you will find on the website. Once you have pressed it, the platform will ask you which blockchain you want to use. At the time of writing, Ethereum, Flow, and Tezos were available. Depending on which blockchain you choose, the process may look slightly different now. I'll describe the steps based on the "Ethereum" selection, as this appeals to potentially the largest group of buyers (but will also likely be the most expensive). If you choose this blockchain, the next question will be to connect by using a wallet. I choose my Metamask account for this purpose.

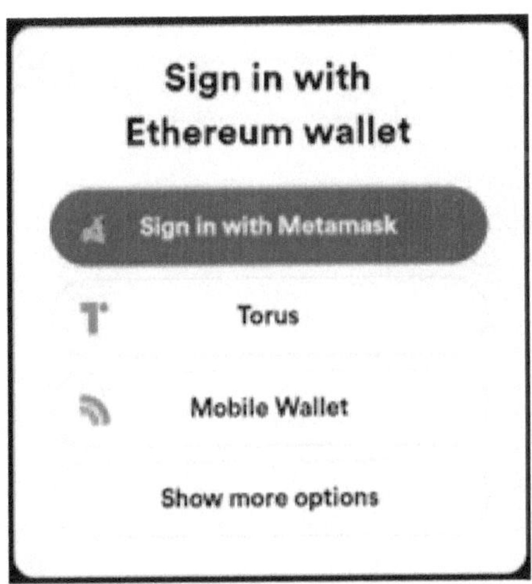

A Metamask wallet window opens and I am offered my Ethereum wallets in Metamask to choose from. Since I only have one, the selection is limited.

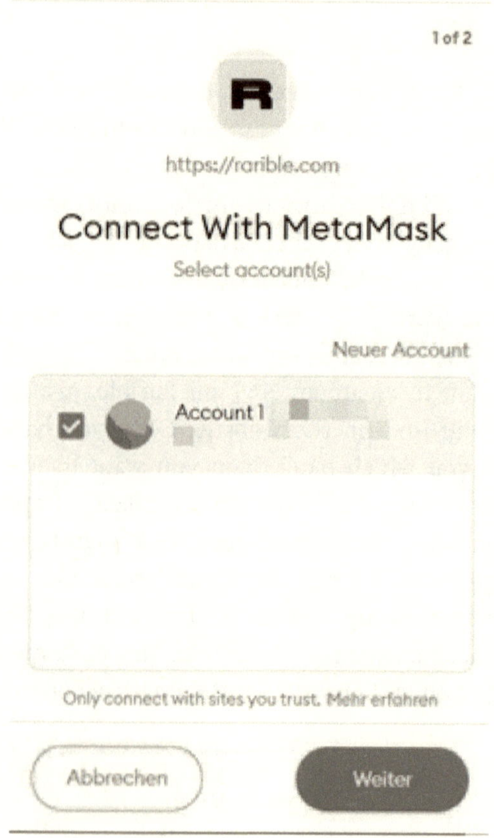

You must then confirm that you are at least 13 years old and accept the T&Cs.

Rarible Terms of Service

Please take a few minutes to read and understand Rarible Terms of Service. To continue, you'll need to accept the Terms of Service by checking the box.

■ I am at least 13 years old

■ I accept the Rarible Terms of Service

Proceed

Sign out

Now you are logged in and can select whether you want to create a Single or a Multiple Item. A Single Item creates a single NFT with the corresponding file. With a Multiple Item, you can select a corresponding edition (this is similar to creating a print with an edition of 100 copies, for example). In this case, the Single Item will probably be more valuable than an Multiple. On the other hand, the sum of multiples may bring you more revenue than a single work and make more interested parties happy. But in any case, it depends on your type of art, your goal and your market.

Choose Type

Choose "Single" for one of a kind or "Multiple" if you want to sell
one collectible multiple times

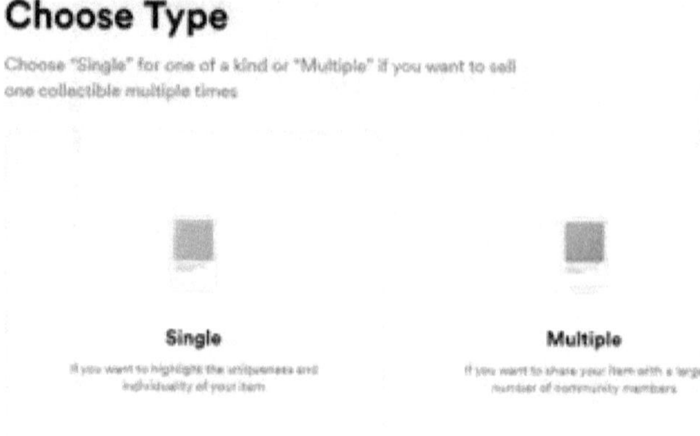

Let's take a closer look at the "single" path together.

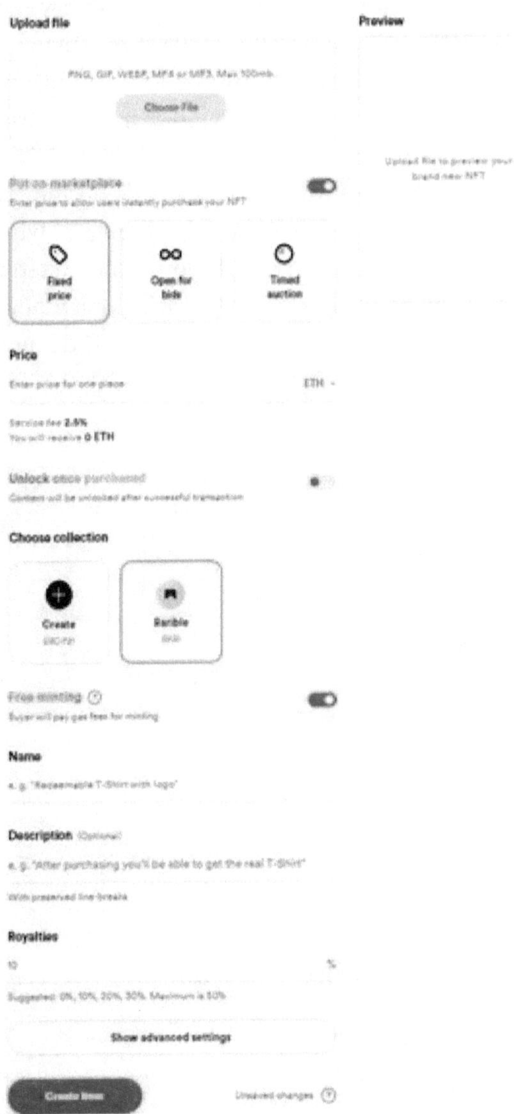

On this page you can now create your NFT. To do this, let's take a closer look at the individual fields:

- **Upload File** - Here you can upload your file. The available file formats (PNG, GIF, WEBP, MP4 or MP3) and the maximum file size (100 MB) are fixed. If you have other file formats, you would have to change them beforehand (e.g. MOV to MP4 or JPEG to PNG or GIF).
- **Upload Cover** - This field appears only after a file has been uploaded. Here you can upload the corresponding cover image. It can be created in JPG, PNG, GIF or WEBP and must not exceed 100 MB.
- **Put on Marketplace** - If you have selected this option, you can decide whether you want to offer your NFT at a fixed price or whether you want the "open for bids" or auction variant. If you want a fixed price, you will then enter your fixed price and the appropriate currency (for example, Ethereum) enter. From this, the marketplace will deduct a service fee when selling, which will be shown.

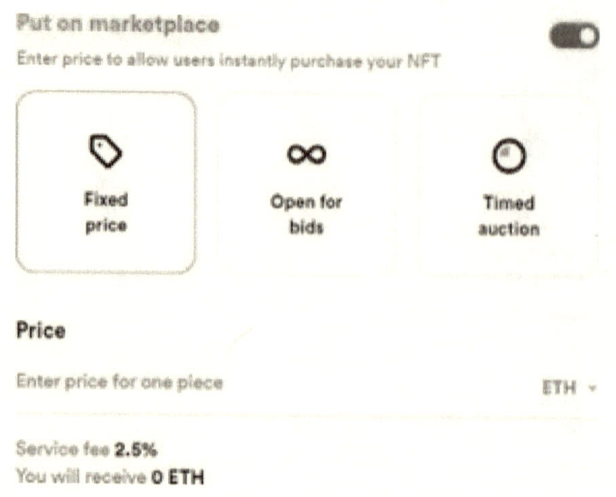

Enter Caption

- If you select "Open for Bids", you will be notified when there are bids for the NFT and can then decide whether to accept them. Of course, appropriate fees will then apply as well.
- In the "Timed Auction" variant, the start date, the auction duration and the minimum price are entered. Only if this minimum price was reached or exceeded, a knockdown will take place. If the highest bid is lower than the minimum price, you can decide whether to accept

this bid anyway.

- **Chose Collection** - The easiest way to explain a collection is to compare it to a folder on your desktop. By default, when you create art on Rarible, the art is placed in either the ERC721 or ERC1155 Rarible folder. This folder is a public folder where anyone is allowed to create NFTs. When you create your own collection, you are essentially creating your own folder where no one but you can create NFTs. Having your own folder can be especially useful if you want to display it on other platforms. For simplicity's sake, I'll go with the Rarible option here.

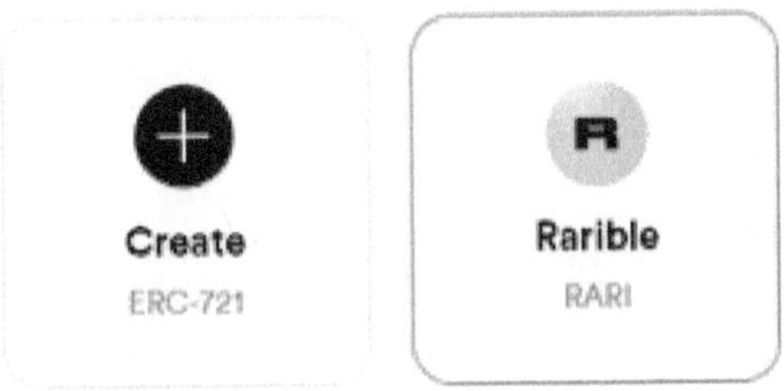

- **Free minting** - Here you can specify whether you want to enter your artwork directly into the blockchain and pay a corresponding gas fee for it, or whether you simply want to store the artwork on the platform and have it entered into the blockchain by a buyer first. The latter, of course, leads to the fact that

additional costs will be incurred by a possible buyer, which he will include in his calculation; on the other hand, you will not incur any costs in this way. In this case, however, the NFT is actually not yet an NFT, but only becomes one upon the first sale.

- The next fields are largely self-explanatory. You can decide whether you want to use all the fields in the Advanced Settings with optional details, or if you only want the minimum details. Make sure that the description is informative and attractive for the potential buyer. A special field is the

"**Royalties**" field. In this field you can name what share you want to have in future sales. I will describe this point in more detail below.

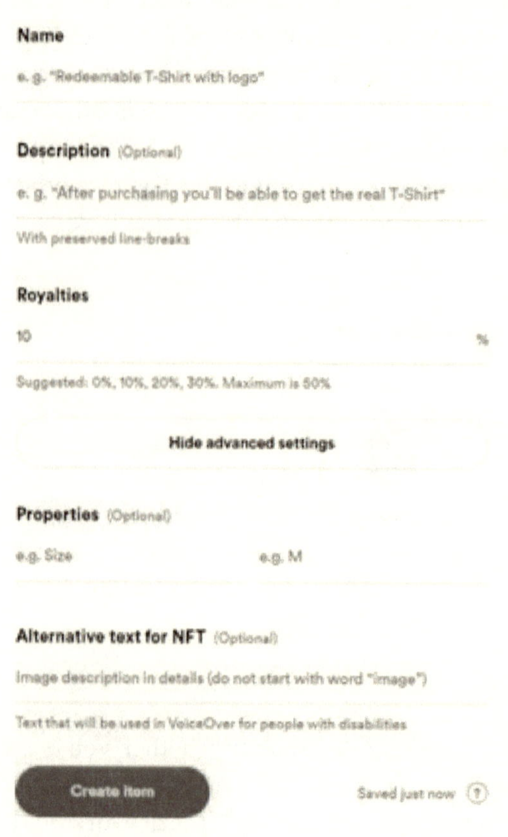

* Once all entries have been made, you can select "Create Item" to create the NFT.

Royaltys

One particular advantage of NFTs has not even come up yet. When selling NFTs, most platforms allow you to specify that you want Royaltys from further sales. This can be capped depending on the platform. Rarible, for example, allows you a royalty share of no more than 50%, while others are sometimes considerably lower. So what does this mean? If you are an art creator and you create a physical work, then in most cases it will be the case that you sell it at a certain point in time. In return, you will receive a sales price, from which costs such as commissions from galleries, etc. may be deducted. After that the work will find a new owner and possibly the value of this work will increase with time. This pleases your client, because he may be able to sell the work you created for a higher price. You get nothing out of it except the satisfaction of having your art appreciated.

If you do something similar in the context of NFT, you may have set a royalty share of, say, 10%. Now, if your customer resells the work you created at a later date, you will automatically find 10% of the sale price in your wallet. This is because the NFT is based on a smart contract approach, in which it is stored that with every further sale, the corresponding payout to you will automatically occur. This happens not only once, but again with every further sale. You receive the share of the sales price, not of the profit. This means that if the buyer sells the NFT you created below its purchase price, you still get 10% of the lower selling price, even though he makes a loss on the investment.

Of course, the marketplaces also show which royalties are associated with the offered works. If, for example, an investor has to be prepared for you to offer a work with a royalty setting of 50%, then he will include this in his calculation. Conversely, this means that he will have to more than double his purchase price in order to make any profit at all. Serious investors will probably shy away from this risk. On the other hand, royalty rates in the lower range, such as 5% or 10%, are something most investors can live with. To get a feel for this, look around the various marketplaces and decide which royaltys make sense for your works.

Opensea.io

We have already looked at the procedure for creating NFTs in Rarible.com. Now let's look together at the corresponding procedure in what is claimed to be the largest marketplace for NFTs. It is the company Opensea.io, which has attracted attention in recent months due to significant growth in terms of goodwill. For example, on January 6, 2022, the BBC headlined, "NFT marketplace OpenSea valued at more than $13bn."[7]. So we are undoubtedly dealing with a major player in the market, which also means that the user can assume that he is dealing with a serious provider and that his investment or his NFTs are also safe in the longer term.

As already mentioned earlier, a major difference between Opensea and other platforms is that a gas fee only has to be paid for the upload of the first NFT. Subsequently, further NFTs can be uploaded free of charge. The corresponding fees are then only incurred upon sale.

However, it is to be said that there are probably considerations to limit the number of "free" NFTs at Opensea in the future. If this is of importance for your decision for a platform, it is certainly worthwhile to check this before posting NFTs on the platform to be verified again on the basis of the conditions of the marketplace presented at the relevant time.

Again, the work starts with you creating an account by selecting "Create". First, you need to connect to your wallet for identification. Opensea supports a variety of wallets here. However, Metamask is preferred:

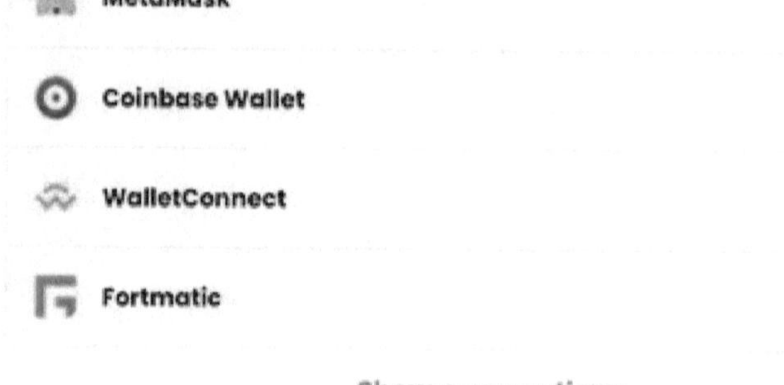

If you do not have any NFTs on the website yet, you will be taken directly to the option to create an NFT.

Create New Item

On the Opensea.io site, unlike Rarible, other file formats such as JPG files are also welcome. Specifically these are: JPG, PNG, GIF, SVG, MP4, WEBM, MP3, WAV, OGG, GLB, GLTF and the maximum size accepted is also 100 MB. After uploading, you can name your NFT and include an external link. This is recommended if, for example, you have created more info about your NFT on an external site that you want to show to potential customers. Maybe a video about the creation process, maybe a presentation of the thoughts and statements associated with your artwork, or possibly a link to your profile as an art creator. The possibilities are very diverse. In any case, the link will be included as part of the presentation. An additional benefit of this link is of course that you will have an incoming link from Opensea.io on the linked page, which may also be positive in the context of search engine ranking optimization.

In the description field you can enter a simple text, but you can also use Markdown tags. You can find a more detailed description of this on the website: https://www.markdownguide.org/cheat-sheet/. This helps to make the text more readable and attractive. Later, when you have your own collections, you can assign the NFT to one of them if you want.

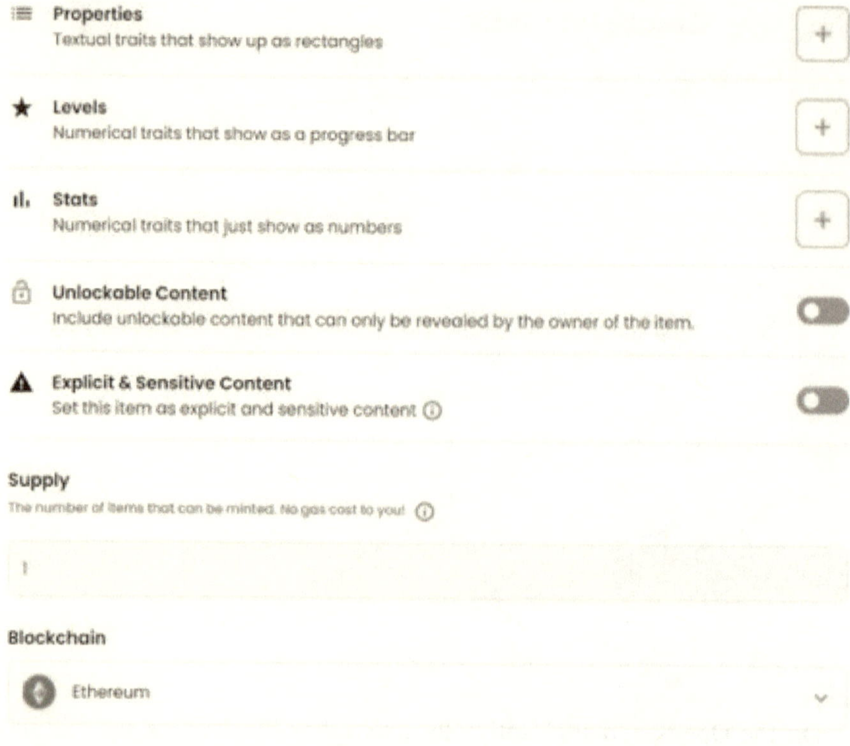

In the following section, additional attributes can be created. You can also specify whether the content is accessible to everyone or can only be shown by the owner and whether the display may contain content that requires special handling (for example, with regard to youth protection). Finally, you specify how many NFTs are to be mined from this file. This is about the question if you want only one original copy or if you want to offer a collection of several files (as for example with print graphics).

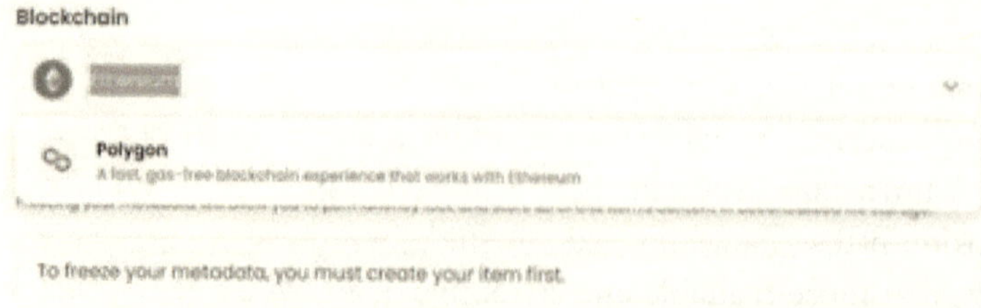

Next, you can specify whether the transaction should take place on the Ethereum or Polygon blockchain. Unlike Ethereum, Polygon is not associated with a gas fee, but also has a considerably smaller customer group.

Once you have uploaded the file, you will be taken to a representation of your work and can now offer it for sale if you wish. To do this, select the "Sell" option.

If you want to continue editing the existing file, you can press "Edit" to return to the edit mode.

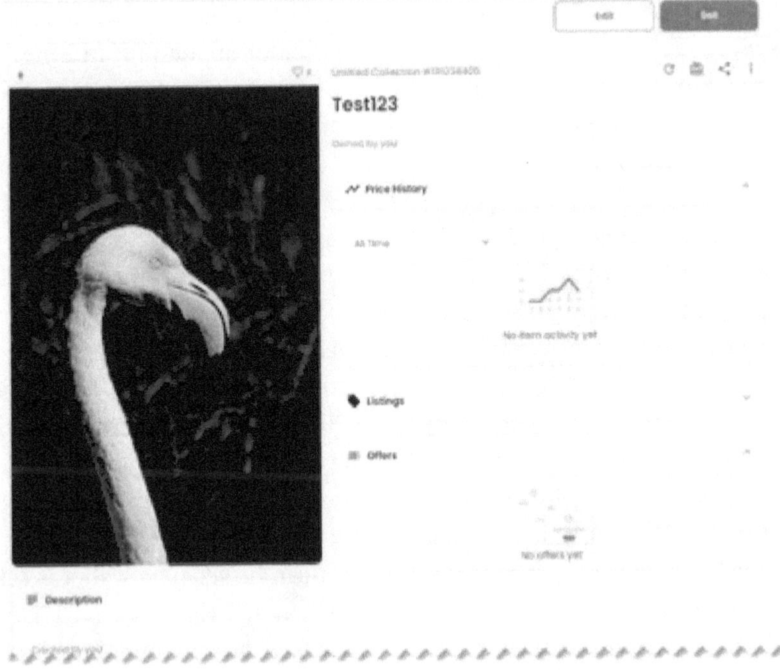

In the "Sell" area you can now choose how you want to offer your work. You can choose between Fixed Price and a Timed Auction, where the highest bidder wins. However, you have the option of setting a minimum bid to ensure that your offer is not accepted for less than the price you have set.

With the fixed price offer, a fixed selling price in Ether and the offer duration can be set. The mentioned 2.5% fees will only be deducted from the selling price when a sale is made. If you enter an amount in Ether, the current daily value in US$ is automatically displayed as additional info, since most sellers can imagine more under US$ amounts than under Ether.

In the auction tab you can specify whether you want to sell at the highest price. You then specify the starting price and the auction duration. If you select "Reserve price", you can still set a minimum price for the fall of the hammer. On the other hand, if you select "Sell with declining price", you set a starting price and a minimum price. The offer will then start with the starting price and as soon as someone bids it, the offer will be knocked down. If no one bids on it, the price will be slowly reduced until final lowered to the minimum price. Here the buyer is: The first one gets it at the current price ... so the longer the buyer waits, the cheaper it becomes, but the more he also risks that another buyer is faster ...

Once the data has been entered, the offer can be set. The wallet is called up again and the gas fee is debited from the first listing. The NFT is now listed on the marketplace and can be purchased by customers. If desired, you can also adjust the entered data at a later time.

However, you should keep in mind that an offer that changes constantly may not look very professional to customers. Therefore, it is worthwhile to create a good offer with the appropriate texts from the very beginning.

Create collections

An important topic when creating NFTs in the Opensea.io platform is creating collections. You can access your collections through "My

Collections".

Now that you have created an NFT first, there will simply be a dummy entry with the existing NFT in the corresponding page. You should edit this. It is virtually the framework for your NFT and as it is in "real life", it also has a noticeable influence on the sales success. In addition, you can regulate some other elements within the collection, which are important if you want to generate sustainable sales and income with your NFTs.

First, you will be asked for three images, which will be used to represent the collection in different contexts. I recommend you to prepare them directly in the correct formats as mentioned in the additional texts on the upload form. You will usually achieve a better and controlled image quality than if another image size is reduced by the page to the required dimension.

As with the NFT, you should again assign a suitable title and a description that is as meaningful as possible and - if available - a link to an external page that possibly explains the collection further.

Edit My Collection

Then you should assign the collection to a category. In doing so, record what type of content the collection is. This will help buyers who collect NFTs of a certain type, for example, to find their way around better. For this reason, it's a good idea to keep collections as single-variety as possible. For example, if you create graphic art and photography, in most cases it makes sense to put them in different categories.

You have the possibility to add more links to your collection. On the one hand, this provides networking and, on the other hand, it also gives your potential customers more identification potential with you, if they can perceive you better as an artist - which will possibly lead to purchases sooner.

Next comes a very important field. It's called "Creators Earnings" and corresponds to what we learned about in Rarible under "Royalties". What you see here can affect whether you receive the sales price less costs only once when you sell a work, or whether you benefit from a percentage of the sales price each time you resell the work.

Unlike Rarible, Opensea currently has a maximum approach of 10%. In my opinion, this is reasonable, because otherwise a buyer will think twice about investing in a work where he will tend to pay more when reselling it - because the share he has to deduct from the sales price is too high. In this case, the strategy of betting on the fact that a work sells several times and that one then has a share in each further sale is more worthwhile.

After that, you will still choose the type of tokens (currency) that will be used to accept payments and the way you want your collection to be displayed. Finally, you should if your content contains special content that is important, for example, in the context of the protection of minors.

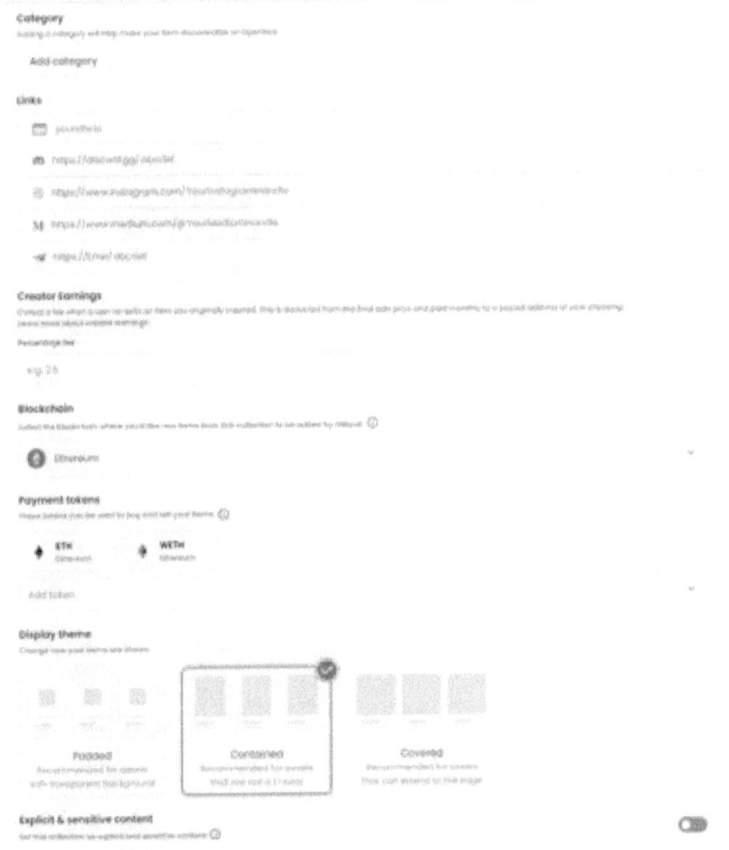

Once you have completed your collection, you can save it. It can also be further adapted and optimized at a later time if required.

Build profile

Potential buyers of an NFT will generally also want to take a closer look at the provider's profile. Accordingly, it is important that the profile is also professionally structured.

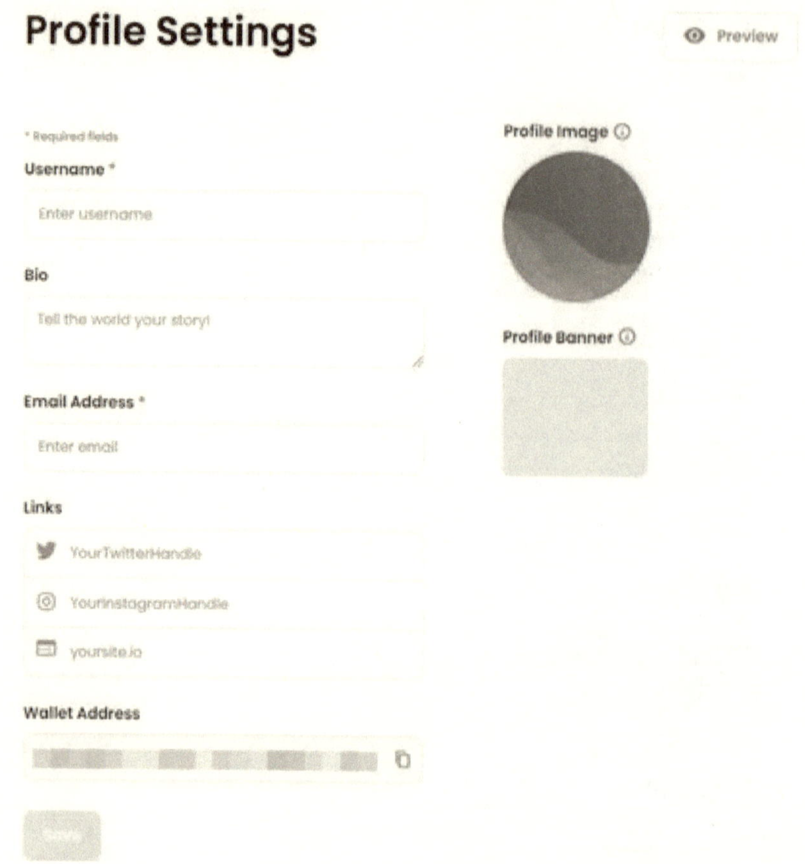

The entries here are self-explanatory. You can of course freely decide whether you want to offer under your birth name or use a pen name or project name. If you do not want to use your birth name or do not want to make it transparent, you should of course also make sure that it cannot be read from your e-mail address or in the context of the linked websites.

Take inspiration for your presentation from other, successful providers in your field. The point is not to copy them. You are unique as an art creator and so should be your external presentation in profile, collections, works and linked pages, but it can of course help to see what successful providers are doing and be inspired by their success measures.

From experience, it is helpful to develop an entire branding around your NFTs to interact with your potential customers. We will discuss this topic further in a later section of the book.

Mintable.app

Now let's look at a third platform. This is Mintable.app. Currently, the main text on the page reads, "Mint your NFT on the Blockchain for Free! - Find it. Buy it. Flip it."

Unlike the aforementioned platforms, Mintable.app offers free minting of NFTs. Since this is very attractive for many providers, the offer on this site is correspondingly large and many NFTs are offered at extremely low prices. You can definitely find offers for literally penny amounts. However, this does not mean that offers in the range of over a thousand euros do not exist and are partly also purchased. It only means that if you want to be sustainably successful in this marketplace, you have to distinguish yourself in a special way from the thousands of other offers. This can be done by the offered work, or - and this is usually more sustainable and promising - by a loyal fan community, which not only appreciates a certain work, but also wants to buy more works.

Unlike many other platforms, an account is created here by entering an e-mail address and password and verified by entering a verification code sent by e-mail. Only then is a connection made to the wallet (for example, Metamask).

To mine a new NFT, press the "Mint" button in the menu bar. A window will pop up asking if the file in question already exists or needs to be created.

DOES YOUR ITEM ALREADY EXIST?

Is the item live on the blockchain or is it a new item you want to make?

The NFT is already in my wallet

Create a new item

Here you will now go to "Create a new Item" and will then again receive a display confirming that there are no transaction costs for this.

You will then be asked which blockchain you want to mine the NFT on.

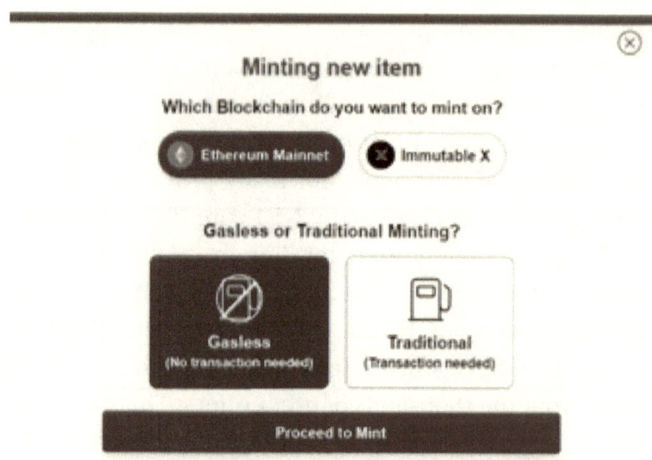

Here you can now choose between the Ethereum blockchain (we have already talked about this several times) and the Immutable X blockchain. If you choose Ethereum, you can either choose "Gasless" (in which case there are no transaction fees and the NFT is only mined for a fee when it is sold) or "Traditional" (in which case, however, there are no transaction fees). Gas-Fees an). Alternatively, you can also select Immutable X. There, only the

Gasless approach is available.

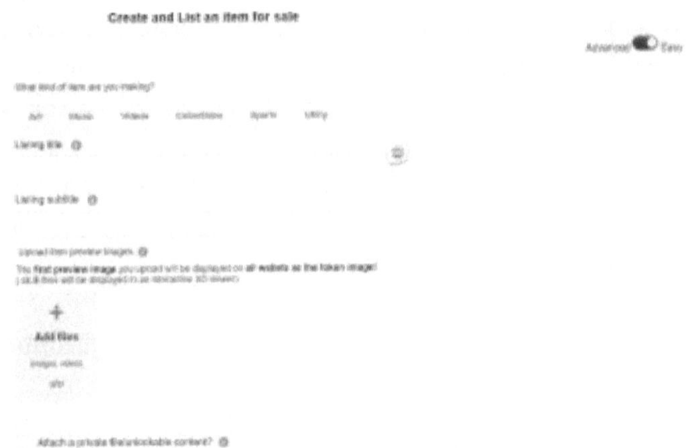

When capturing new NFTs, you can choose between advanced functions (fields that form additional additions to the description) and an Easy capture, which only queries the necessary field contents. As a file you can choose a variety of image, video and animation files (e.g. animated gifs). Here, too, you can choose between fixed price offers and auctions. In the case of the auction offer, there is an additional option of combining it with a "Buy Now" function, which allows buyers to buy directly during an ongoing auction if they select the "Buy Now" amount. Otherwise, the revenues are comparable to those of the aforementioned platforms.

What still needs to be done

Now we have talked a lot about how an NFT can be mined, i.e. entered in the blockchain and offered for sale on platforms. However, some readers may ask themselves how they can create an NFT in the first place or how they can select from their existing works those that are suitable as NFTs and also have a chance of being successfully sold via one of the aforementioned - or one of the many other - platforms.

NFTs make it possible to offer and market a completely new kind of art or art products. Depending on the setting, the NFT technology can play an important part in the work or merely represent a carrier technology. We will take a closer look at some approaches to this in the section on various success stories.

As you have probably already gathered from the previous chapters, technically all kinds of digital data are capable of being linked to NFTs, and there are even approaches to using NFTs in a combination of digital and analog worlds as well. However, in this book we will at least stay with NFTs in the digital context. Possible files/data are: images, videos, audio files, 3D models, texts and domains, to name only the most common ones.

If you are thinking about which files you would like to offer as NFT, you should first ask yourself a few questions:

ax. For whom do I create the NFTs, who are my potential customers?

ax. Do it for themselves, for their fans ...

ax. Do I only want to earn money with the NFTs or do I also want to use them as a retention tool for my fans? (other reasons are possible)

ax. Why should customers buy my NFTs of all things?

ax. Do I have a special bond with my potential customers?

ax. What additional benefit (besides owning a picture) am I possibly offering buyers?

ax. What benefit / goal are my buyers pursuing with their purchase?

ax. Do I have to do the whole thing on my own or does it make sense to set something up in cooperation with others, if applicable?

ax. Could the NFT possibly be part of something bigger?

ax. What are my own expectations of an NFT?

ax. What is my expectation when offering NFTs?

Depending on your answers to the above questions, your approach and the works you offer may look very different.

Let's look at a few possible ideas in this context:

ax. Possession of one of your NFTs may perhaps entitle you to be invited to a particular concert as a guest or, if applicable, to interact with you as part of an online session.

ax. Perhaps offer NFT holders the opportunity to attend certain events at special NFT rates.

ax. Perhaps the NFT is associated with a corresponding mention as a sponsor on your website.

ax. Perhaps the NFT offers the basis for membership in a special fan community.

There are endless possible ideas and approaches. Before you start uploading lots of random files to platforms, you should seriously consider what your buyer will get out of their purchase. It has been shown that NFTs that are not just about making a quick buck, but provide real value to buyers, are the most successful and sustainable. But to do that, you need to think from your buyers' point of view. To use a common saying here, "The bait must be to the fish's liking, not the angler's."

[1] If you would like to find out more about this, you should read up on the topic of distributed ledger technology. However, an in-depth understanding of the technology is not necessary for its use, which is why we will refrain from elaborating on the subject here.

[2] I will spare you the technical basics of proof of work and proof of stake here. If you are interested, you will find plenty of further information on the Internet.

[3] https://www.forbes.com/advisor/investing/best-crypto-exchanges/

[4] we discuss these in more detail in a subsequent chapter

[5] Attention: The amount and general conditions regarding gas fees are constantly changing. In any case, always observe the current conditions of a platform as they are at the time of your activity.

[6] there is no reason not to do both

[7] https://www.bbc.com/news/technology-59880739

CHAPTER THREE

Success stories from practice

The following examples are just a few of many that have achieved a certain notoriety in recent months. Partly because they have attracted attention through special individual sales, partly because of the success of an entire portfolio of works. But these are by no means the only successes. It should also be said that, in addition to these "stars" of the NFT industry, there are also a huge number of people who simply earn a steady income with NFT in the range of a few hundred or thousand euros a month. Becoming one of them is possible in any case. Of course, the path to the top earners will be reserved for only a few.

Beepl

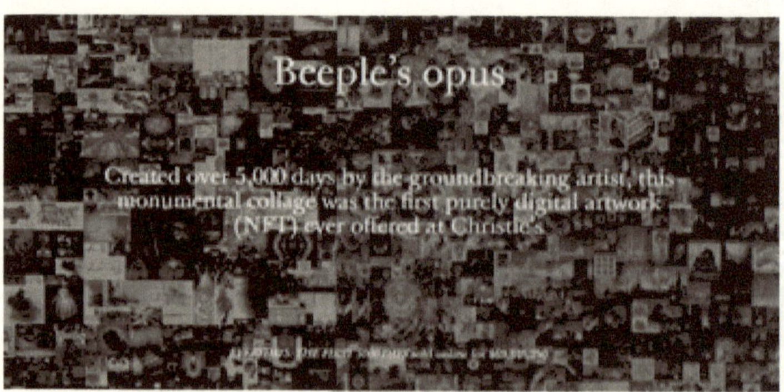

[1]

In over 5000 days, the artist Beeple created a monumental digital collage, which was the first purely digital artwork with an NFT approach to be offered at Christie's and eventually sold for over US$69 million. If you convert this to 5000 days, the artist earned 13 800 US$ per working day, which he worked on the picture and even if you calculate that it could have been a few days more and the auction house also deducted fees, we still come to a daily earnings, which some people do not earn with their art even in several months.

Subsequently, there was a lot of discussion about the question whether what Beeple has created here is really art. This may be judged differently and that should not be our topic here. The fact is that there were apparently several people who were of the opinion that the work was indeed valuable. A painting can only achieve such a high price in an auction if at least two parties absolutely want to own it.

What can we learn from this example? Even though we probably don't expect - and probably shouldn't - that our works will sell for comparable prices, most artists would be quite satisfied with even a fraction of the hammer price.

The basis for such success is to be perceived by people as a creator of art and to create a corresponding community that is interested in the works (and the person). Beeple has achieved this, among other things, through a large community of followers in social media.

- https://www.instagram.com/beeple_crap/ - about 2.5 million followers
- https://twitter.com/beeple - just under 600,000 followers https://beeple.tumblr.com/

- https://www.facebook.com/beeple - over 600 000 followers

- https://www.youtube.com/beeple - over 61 000 subscribers and likes on individual videos up to ¼ million. etc.

With this presence, the artist has established himself over the years and has become his own "brand". This in turn leads to the fact that the artist was not only able to sell a work once, but, for example, on Nifty Gateway continuously sells pictures and with "normal" works is currently traded at a street price of about $ 60 000 per work. Which, of course, does not mean that each of his paintings "sells like hot cakes".

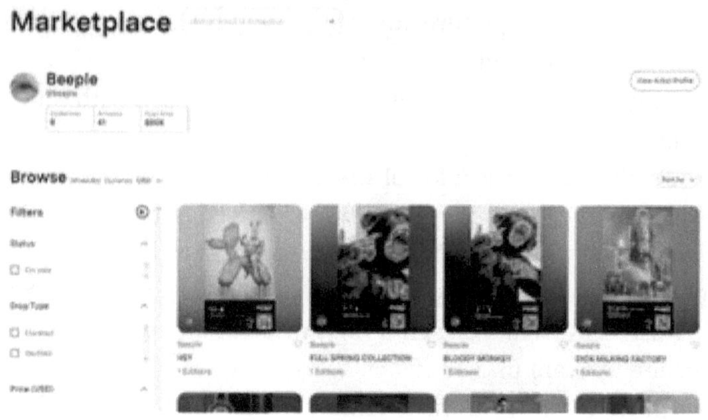

Enter Caption

[2]

Beeple has worked on Nifty Gateway for a long time with different editions. In addition to single editions, i.e. works with an edition of "1", which he offered in auctions, he also offered open editions, for example. During a certain time (5 minutes), any number of works could be purchased at a fixed price. These then also consisted not only of a file, but of a gift box, which contained the token and other special elements (e.g. his hair - thus a part of him) and was delivered to the buyers within a few weeks after the auction. Finally, he offered $1 editions in a limited run of 100 pieces. In doing so, the $1 collections are big business for the vendor, as he participates in every resale through Royaltys (we've talked about this) and thus - by giving his fans the opportunity to make a lot of money - also participates in every sale in turn.

This mixture led to the fact that it was possible on the one hand to acquire unique works for expensive money (investor), to own special editions, which one could also show physically (status), as well as to own a share as a fan, which was already included in the moment you bought it was worth more than what you paid for it (**investor, admirer, pragmatic buyer**).

This then also results in such offers:

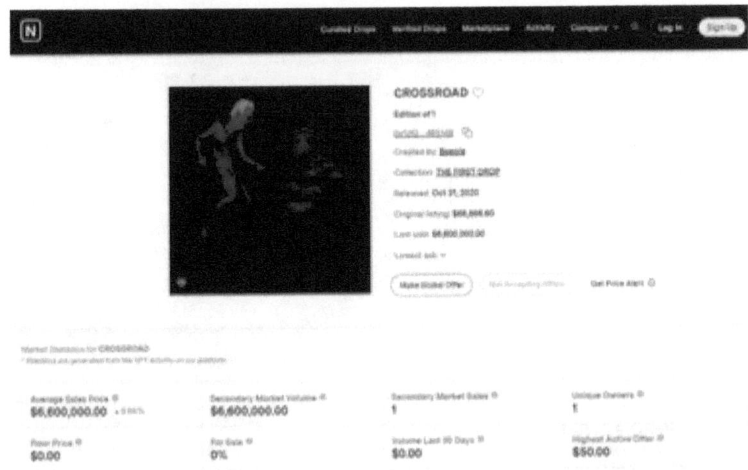

[3]

The present offer was originally sold for $ 66 666.60, and the last sold for $ 6.6M. Of course, not every one of his works made such profits.

Let's now summarize a few key success factors:

- The artist built a community.
- The artist did what he loved, is thereby also sustainably active and constantly develops his community.
- The artist let people participate in his development as an artist and in the development of artworks (relationship building).
- The artist offered works that appeal to very different groups of buyers.
- The artist has found a way to break through the digital-only market by creating a physical set that appeals to people who might have been reluctant to a digital- only work.

Gery Vee NFT Project

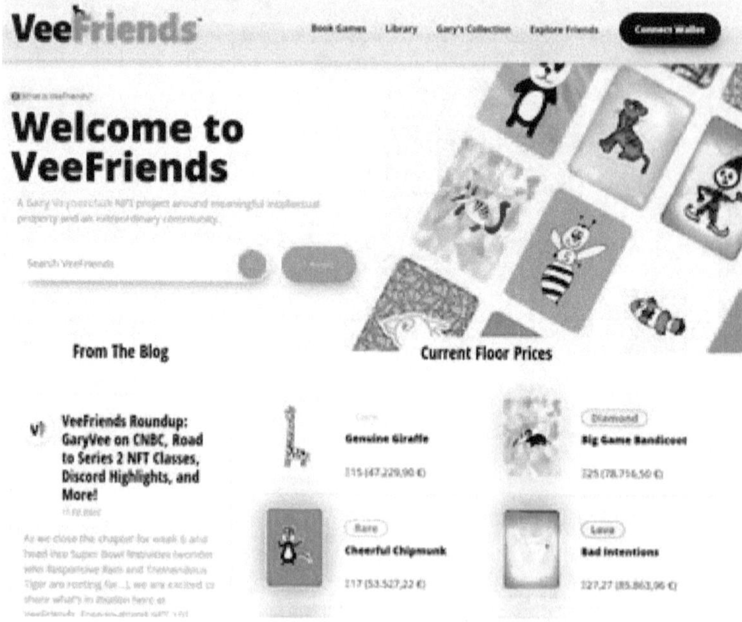

[4]

Another NFT project we want to take a closer look at is VeeFriends. A good introduction to the project can be found on Gary Vee's Youtube channel:

https://www.youtube.com/watch?v=DmDieez1GYQ

If we look at the art of Gary Vee, it is fair to say that his works do not necessarily correspond to a common concept of art:

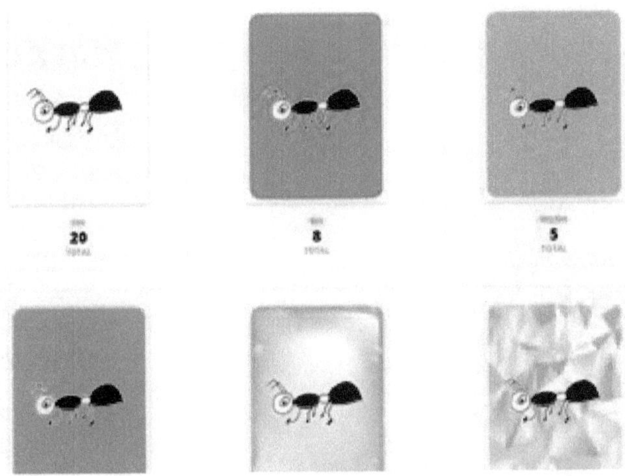

[5]

However, the artist Gary Vaynerchuk himself would hardly say that about his works in this case. Rather, his works are a kind of ticket into a very special community. Here, at the latest, you should also notice that NFT art in many cases encompasses far more than just "art" in the conventional sense. What we also see is that the artist also markets his works on his own platform[6] and thus does not use one of the many marketplaces, which in turn means considerably more effort, but of course also leads to having more independence and not having to pay percentages to the marketplace.

If we look a little closer at the example of an offer, we learn more about what the new owner of the NFT is acquiring besides the actual property.

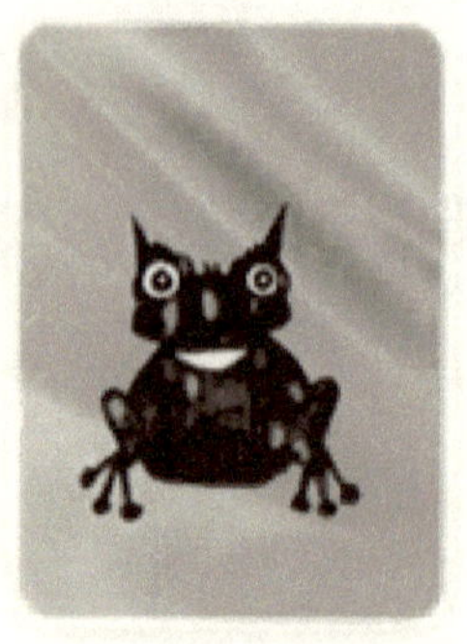

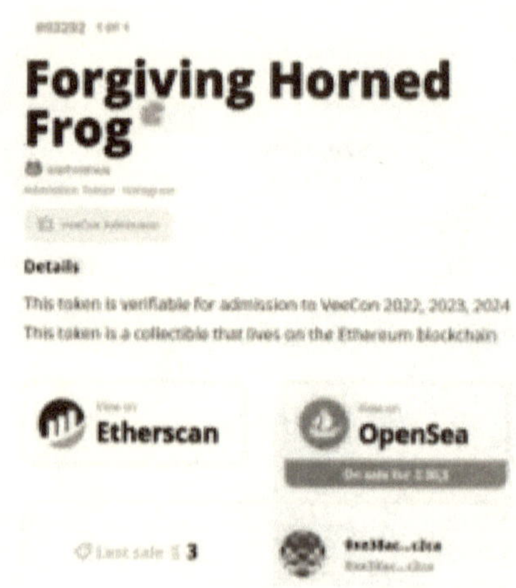

[7]

Thus, access to three VeeCons is co-acquired. Thus, in addition to the actual work of art, it is also a form of admission tickets. On the website you can read (translated):

"All VeeFriends token holders will receive access to VeeCon. VeeCon is a multi-day event exclusively for NFT holders. Your NFT gives you a three-year access pass. The conference focuses on business, marketing, ideas, creativity, entrepreneurship, innovation, competition and, of course, fun. Gary is focused on organizing the best experience for his community and providing tremendous access and information value to all VeeFriends token holders in attendance. If you have two VeeFriends tokens, that means you have two tickets to VeeCon. All dates and locations for VeeCon 2022, 2023, 2024 will be announced at least 180 days in advance. The first VeeCon will be held May 19-22, 2022 in Minneapolis, Minnesota."

In addition, all members of the community can be active in their own virtual community via Discord[8] and exchange information with other members of the community.

Let's now summarize a few key success factors:

- The artist not only builds a "customer" community, but also actively shapes it, thereby achieving customer loyalty.

- The artist is doing something he loves and can accordingly be active in the long term and thus build and expand a community.
- It offers its customers exclusive access to an event that can only be accessed by owning an NFT (status).
- By hosting appropriate events, the artist generates additional publicity and an additional social media presence (attendees who spread the word about their participation on social media and in turn generate publicity for the Making NFTs as access to the next event, press writing about events …)
- Building a community creates a close connection with customers and admirers. Customers are not only owners of art, but also part of a community.

CryptoPunks

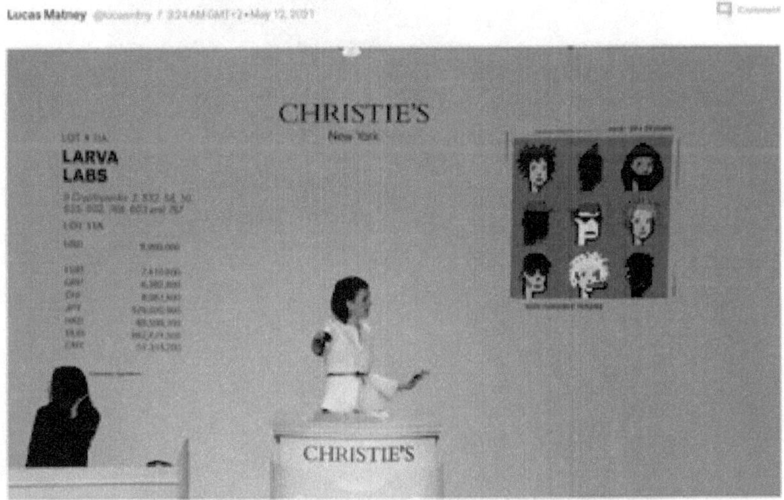

CryptoPunks NFT bundle goes for $17 million in Christie's auction

[9]

Another NFT project that made it into the press is called "CryptoPunks" and 9 of these works were knocked down at Christie's last year for just under US$17 million.

Let's find out together what is the winning formula behind this work and this sales success. Once again, you can't necessarily assume that it's the high artistry of the creator of these nine heads in comic style. But what then leads people to spend millions on works that do not differ significantly from children's drawings? It should be noted that an artist did not create the Cryptopunks directly, but that they were generated by a program with an artificial intelligence (AI) component.

An important reason for the success of this work is certainly that it is one of the first NFTs. Now this "head start" is not something we could imitate or use for our works, or so one would think. In fact, just the opposite is true. We are still in the early days of NFTs and even if some media commentaries today are already talking again about the time of NFTs being over, one may assume that it is similar to Bitcoin or other larger cryptocurrencies. In fact, the market with digital assets is of course also very responsive to political and economic developments. We have already experienced this several times with Bitcoin. However, the trend has always remained upward. One can - but does not have to - assume that NFTs can develop similarly.

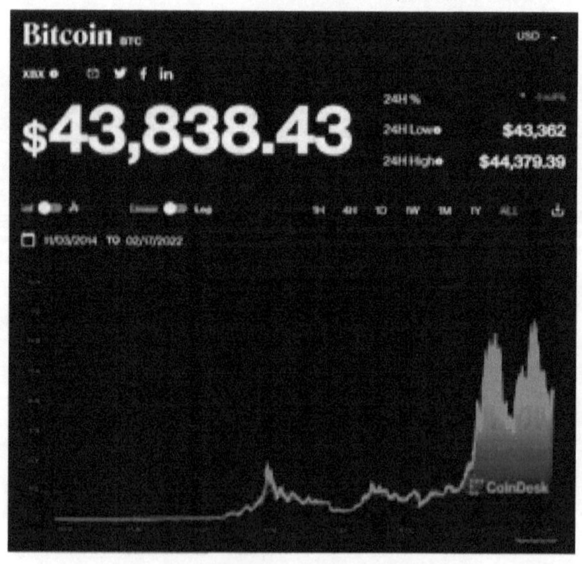

[10]

About the project, the website "The Verge" writes[11] (translated):

"*CryptoPunks were one of the earliest NFT projects and are becoming more valuable as collectibles. The project, launched in 2017 by Larva Labs, offered 10,000 small pixel art portraits of humans, zombies, aliens and apes. Each was generated algorithmically and has different attributes like hairstyle, glasses or hat. Some features are rarer than others, and these tend to yield more valuable CryptoPunks.*

This sale[12] of nine CryptoPunks came from Larva Labs itself. The group initially kept 1,000 of the NFTs for themselves and gave away the rest. The bundle of nine includes a CryptoPunk with a particularly rare feature: CryptoPunk 635, the one with the blue face and sunglasses, is one of only nine "Alien" Punks in the entire series. Another of the nine sold, CryptoPunk 2, the one with wild black hair that looks a bit like a heart, has the distinction of being number two in a series with 10,000 works to be.

CryptoPunks have grown in popularity since the value of NFTs exploded in February. Two Alien Punks sold for more than $7.5 million each in March. Another seven have sold for more than $1 million in recent months."

If we now look at the current statistics at the time of writing on the Larvalabs website, they show some impressive numbers:

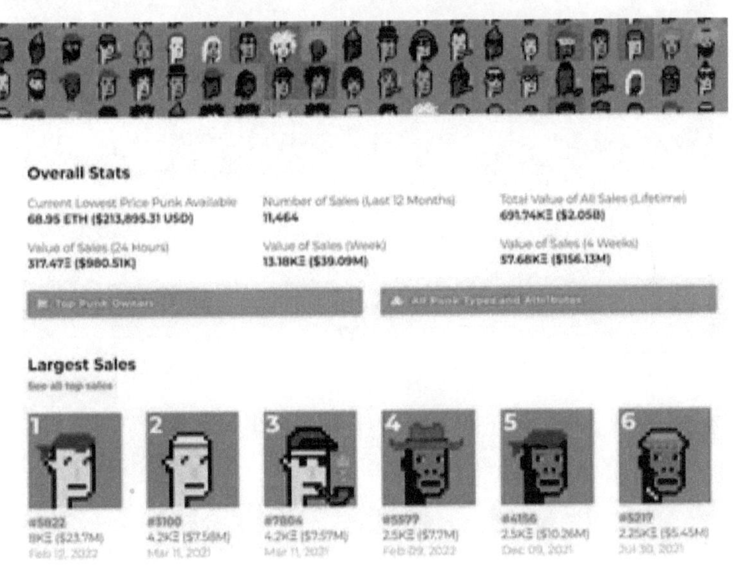

[13]

The current lowest price for offered CryptoPunks was 68.95 ETH, which was equivalent to over US$200,000. There were a total of 11,464 sales and thus a total turnover of over US$2.05 billion was realized. The largest turnover was made by the sale of a CryptoPunk with the number 5822 for the equivalent of US$23.7 million on February 12, 2022[14].

Meanwhile, LavaLabs has released another series, the Meebits (https://meebits.larvalabs.com/). Part of the edition will be given away to existing customers of Cryptopunks and Autoglyph owners (https://larvalabs.com/autoglyphs), the rest will go into the market. The meebits will also be able to be used as avatars in various online platforms. Of the 20,000 Meebits given out, 9,000 are to go into free trade and be sold there, in addition to the ones given away. It can be assumed that again a portion (I estimate 1000) of the work will be held back and offered later only when the value development makes that reasonable.

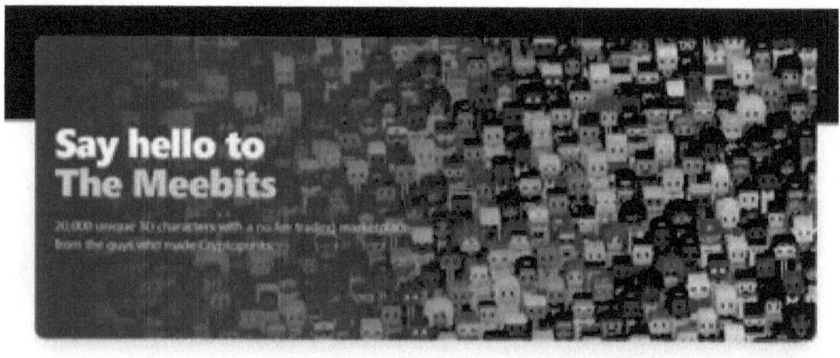

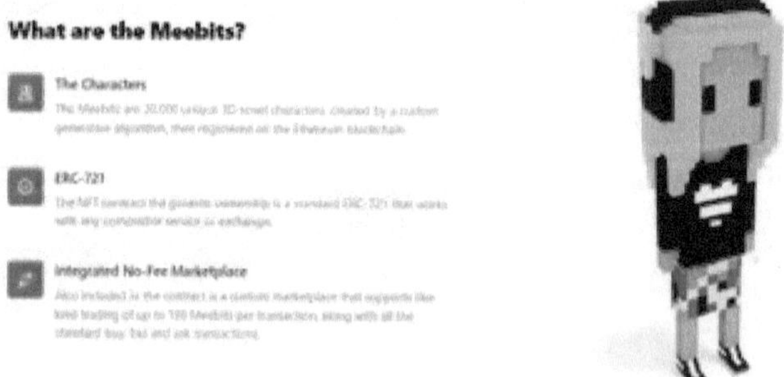

[15]

Let's summarize a few key success factors of CryptoPunks:

- They were very early providers and have thus been on the market and known for a long time.
- They gave a large part of the collection to their fans early on and are now benefiting from the appreciation through Royaltys, which flow to them when they resell based on smart contracts.
- They have retained a certain share of the portfolio and, now that prices have picked up, can offer it at prices that would never have been attainable originally.
- Lava Labs has developed additional market access and factory series, rewards existing owners (community loyalty) and lets them share in the success.
- Of course, the announced gift of the Meebits also leads to a corresponding positive development of the value of the eligible CryptoPunks.

Again, we see that successful NFT projects are not just about a work that is sold, but about building a community and also taking the community and its wishes and needs seriously and letting them participate in the successes.

Kygo

Let's now take a closer look at a completely different project. This time it's about musical art.

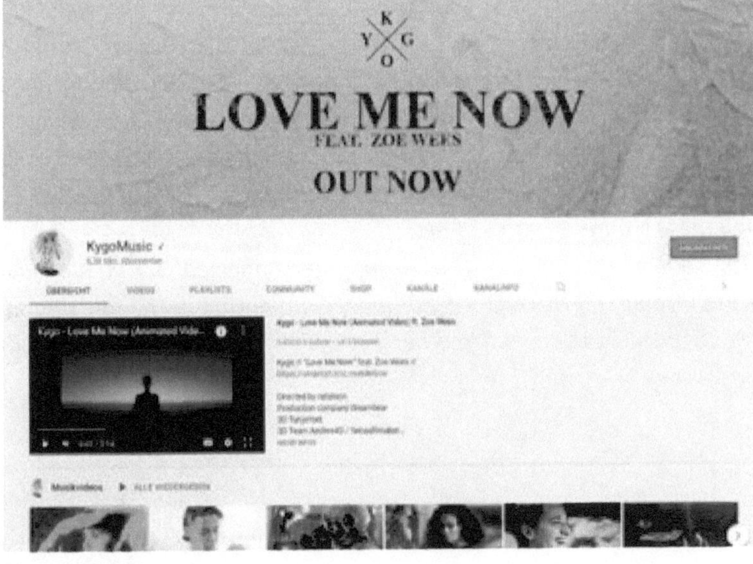

[16]

The Youtube channel of the artist Kygo currently has over 6 million subscribers and if we look at his works, we notice that several of his videos have several 100 million views:

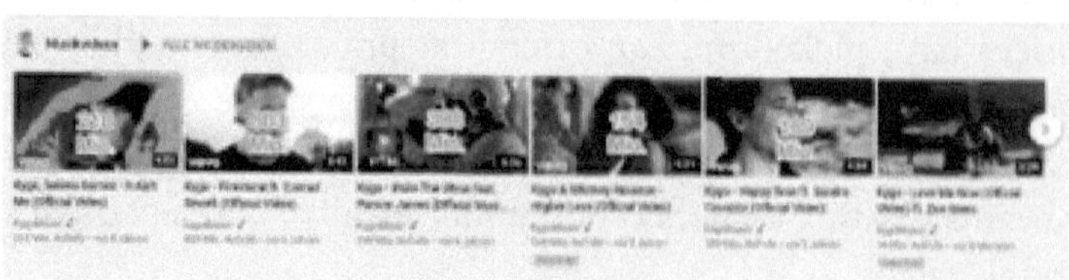

Nifty Gateway, where he offers his works as NFT, writes about it (translated):

"Kygo's story began in 2014 with the world tour "Endless Summer" and since then his journey has not only continued around the globe, it has become a boundless one, leading us to his first NFT collection aptly titled "The Endless Journey." As the musical chapters unfold, art director Simon Evans, who has overseen the visual show design for the past 7 years, continues to collaborate with the Kygo team to create new realms and unlock enchanting worlds with iconic objects that guide us through this picturesque world. As Kygo's debut album is called Cloud 9, the first open editions will only be available for 9 minutes and will include unseen animations from creative design studio Visual Artform and exclusive backstage footage shot by Kygo's video director Johannes Lovund of Palm Tree Productions. These new features show how music, video and digital art combined in true harmony can open the door to a world of endless possibilities where you, the collector, can interpret your own narrative while enjoying these stunning works of art.

"The Endless Journey" is a series of interconnected 3D virtual journeys that wind through all three Open Editions, culminating in the fourth and final journey included in the 1/1 "Another Level," which is meant to symbolize an endless journey."

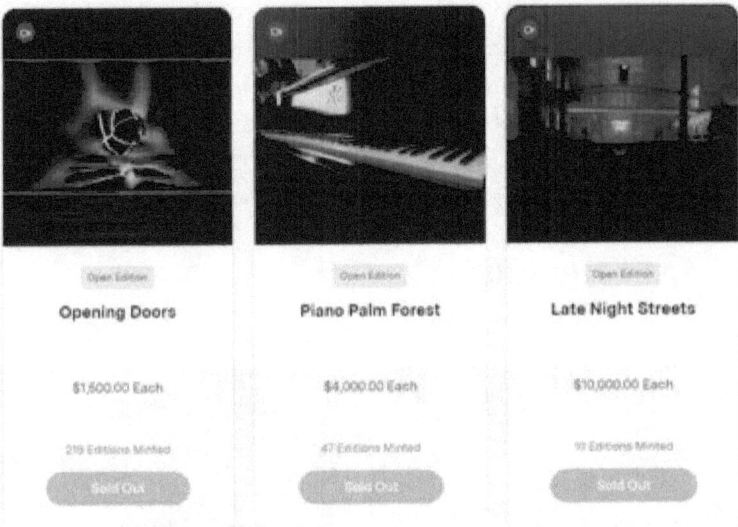

[17]

When we look at offers here, we find that at the current time, prices for these NFTs have dropped in the secondary market. That means owners who want to sell them now will tend to sell below their purchase price. This is certainly not what the artist was aiming for.

Nevertheless, it remains the case that the artist also earns money on the Royaltys, which are in the Smart Contract, when works are resold. Let's assume, for example, that he has set 10% of the sales price as royalty. This means that when he sells an "Open Doors" NFT, he will have earned the original selling price of US$1500, minus the marketplace fees. For example, if a work is now resold below cost by the former buyer for US$1000, the former buyer now gets 90% of the sale price as the seller, and the original creator gets 10%, which is US$100 (all minus fees). This is not a one-time occurrence, but happens with each resale. Therein lies the power of the Royaltys ... Nevertheless, it is in the sense of an artist that the value of his works as NFT does not "collapse".

Let us now look for possible reasons why this drop in value occurred:

ax. After the works were sold, there was no or too little communication about them. The market was not or too little sustainably maintained.

ax. It remained only with the NFTs and, unlike the previously mentioned examples, there was no further benefit that could lead to the possession of the NFTs being of lasting interest. Here, it would be conceivable to grant owners special access to concerts or to include them in a special fan community with which there would be further interaction, etc.

For this, let's look at another example that does a far better job here:

Bored Ape Yacht Club

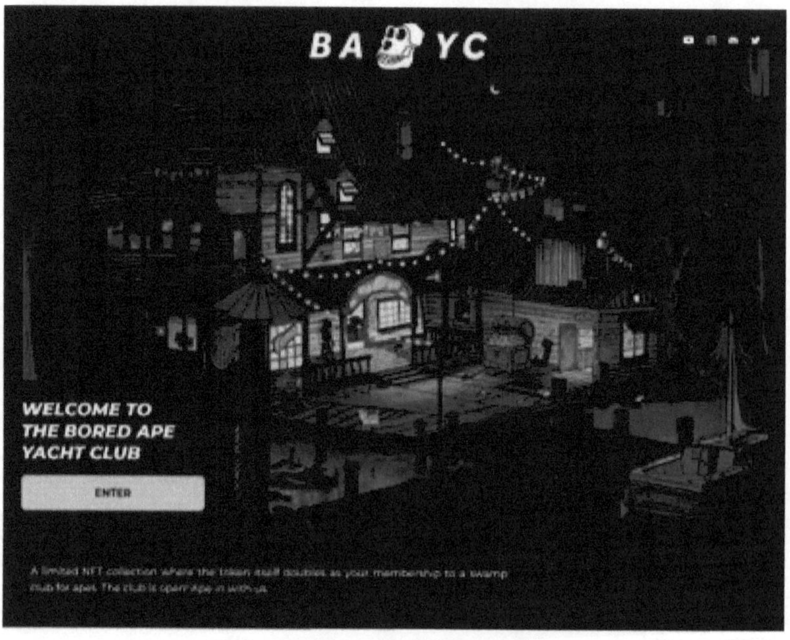

[18]

With the BAYC, or Bored Ape Yacht Club, NFT has finally arrived in the mainstream and is no longer just a topic for a few tech-savvy specialists. Of course, this success story has already reached the big auction world. For example, on September 28, 2021, Christie's, one of the largest international auction houses, sold Ape 8746 at auction for HK$9.61 million, which is equivalent to just under €1.1 million. The bidding stated, among other things, that the image was 631 x 631 pixels and was minted on May 1, 2021.

This results in an exotic price of just under 3 euros per pixel within less than half a year since its creation.

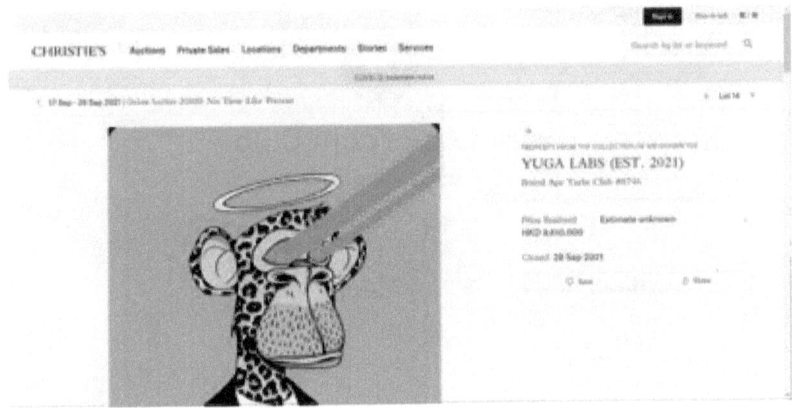

[19]

But what has led to such an increase in value or, in other words, what does this BAYC do that these admittedly interesting-looking drawings achieve such prices (of course, not all do - it is again a matter of rarity, market, etc.)? But even the average Ape is not to be sneezed at in terms of its performance. Currently on Opensea a floor price of 94 Ether is mentioned, which means about 220 000 Euro and that with about 10 000 items and about 6300 owners. This means that - if one were to set the floor price as the standard - the entire Bored Ape family would be worth around 2.2 billion euros, which would make it almost five times more valuable than Leonardo da Vinci's most expensive oil painting to date. Of course, this is a truncated view, since the price would logically drop enormously if 10,000 works were thrown onto the market at the same time.

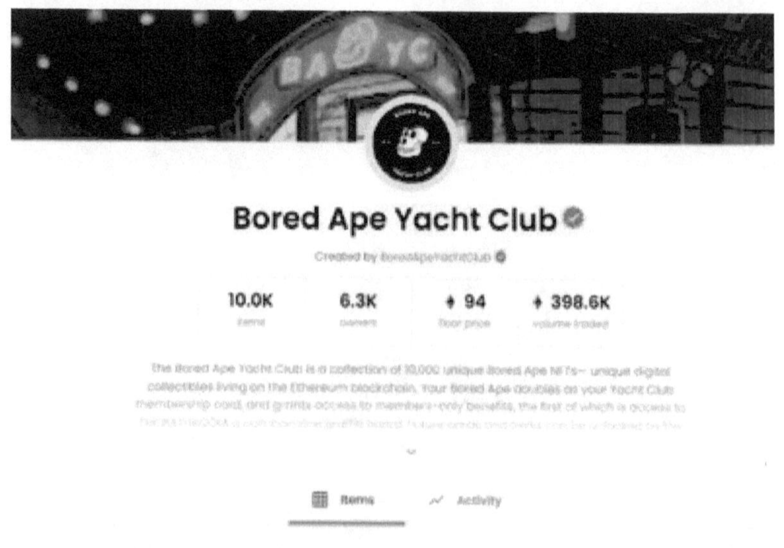

Enter Caption

[20]

In fact, other platforms have sprung up around the Bored Ape theme. The Mutant Ape Yacht Club has been particularly successful. What is happening now is that on Opensea, under "Bored Ape Chemistry Club," a provider is offering three different "serums" that can be used to transform normal bored apes. The three serums are of course also chargeable, depending on how big the transformation to be achieved with them is. To be precise, if the owner of a normal Bored Ape, for example, purchases an M1 serum in addition to his NFT, he will create another (M1) Ape based on his original Ape, as it were, which is a mutation of the original Ape. Thus, the M1 serum holder still owns the original Ape as well as an additional transformed one.

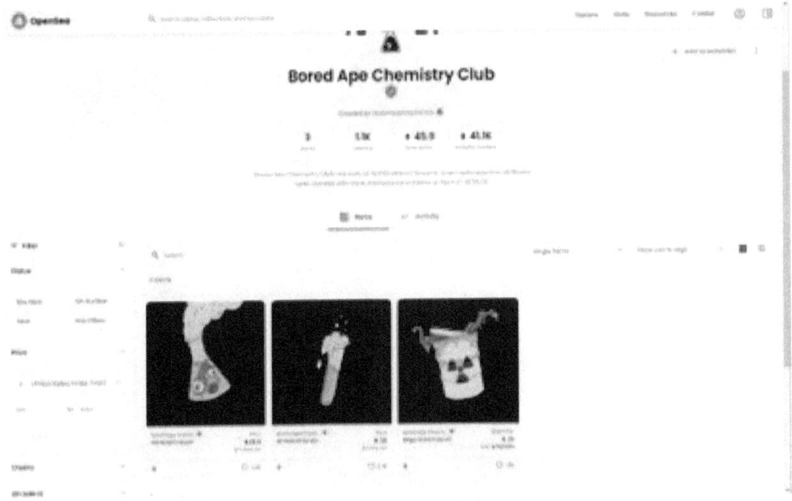

Enter Caption

[21]

These additional Mutant Apes are now offered in the Mutant Ape Yacht Club. The minimum price per mutant ape is still 18 ether, which is currently still over 40,000 euros, and there are currently about 18,000 mutant apes. By the way, the three different serums differ in how much they mutate the ape. The M2 serum is more expensive and rarer, which means that apes mutated with M2 serum also become rarer and more valuable. Of course, the same is even more true for the Mega Mutant Serum.

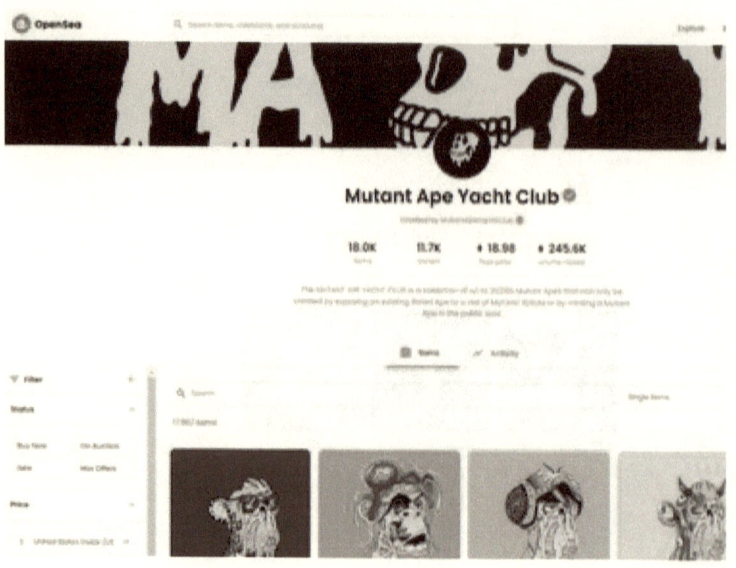

[22]

So what does this mean for customers? For a "small" additional investment, they receive another Ape, which in turn increases in value. On the one hand, the suppliers of the serums sell the serums and on the other hand, they probably also have additional income from the increase in value of the mutant apes via Royaltys. The original producers of the Bored Apes, in turn, have the advantage that their NFTs become more attractive as the ecosystem grows. This in turn leads to further increases in value and better sales, which in turn also benefits them via Royaltys.

Let's see what we can learn from this example beyond what has already been said in other examples:

○ The providers have created an offer for a community and have invested a lot of time in building the community. This has led to the creation of an ecosystem around this community, which offers further benefits and profits to the owners of the NFTs. This in turn boosts the value of the NFTs and thus the attractiveness of the community and the value development of the NFTs, which leads to lively trading with many ever higher Royaltys.

- ◦ Collaborating with other artists with their own ideas has created a classic win-win situation on the part of both suppliers and buyers.

What can we learn from these examples?

Of course, your strategy and market access depend mainly on whether your art appeals to people and motivates them to make a purchase. It is undoubtedly true that different types of art and different groups of buyers have very different needs, desires and decision-making criteria. It is always important to take these into account in an appropriate manner. Finally, it should not be forgotten that a market approach should also correspond to your wishes and your personality as a supplier. For the most part, it will not bring long-term success if you try to bend yourself and your approach to the market in order to attract any customers. For one thing, doing so is unlikely to build long-term client relationships or standing in an appropriate segment of the art market. For another, it may also cause one to lose interest and desire in this market approach oneself and accordingly not use it in the way that would be necessary to be successful. Nevertheless, let's look at a few important success factors that have been useful for art creators:

Fans instead of customers

Many NFT sellers are so intent on finding a customer who will wire them money that they don't think beyond that one-time purchase. In contrast, it has long been known in the business world that it is much less difficult to get an existing customer to make another purchase (assuming they were satisfied) than it is to get a new one. Learn from this, as many successful vendors already do. Find ways to retain existing customers (and, if applicable, buyers of works that they did not purchase directly from you, but from one of your customers). There are various ways to do this: special offers for such people, communities, etc. In the context of NFTs, you also have an increased interest because of the royalties that the secondary market also runs and your customers can in turn resell their works easily and as profitably as possible. This also gives you an ongoing source of income beyond your own sales.

Community

Building a community (which can be a purely virtual community within the context of a platform, such as with the Bored Ape Yacht Club, or a community that also occurs in the "real world," as with Gery Vee) can provide wonderful opportunities for customer engagement.

Another exciting aspect of building a community is that you'll enjoy a completely different reputation by being more closely connected to your community. Take a look at successful artists, singers, musicians, etc. for example. Many of them are very talented, but some are not at all. It is safe to say that it is not necessarily those who have created the best art who are the most successful. Rather, in many cases it is those who have been able to attract a particularly active community.

Pay attention to what these "stars" are doing to retain the community and thus maintain and expand their success in the long term. This is especially true for the new profession of influencers. Many of these people, some of whom earn millions, have no special artistic skills. Their strength and success lie in establishing and maintaining a connection with people. In this way, they create a community that follows them and buys products and services recommended by them.

However, the focus should not be on selling as much as possible, but on achieving benefits for the customer. Your buyers understand very well whether you care about them or whether you are just putting on the whole thing as an extended sales event. Therefore, always put yourself in the position of your buyers: What would you want from an artist - apart from good art?

Think from the buyer

You are probably familiar with the saying that the worm should taste good to the fish and not to the angler. In fact, many artists make the economic mistake of thinking only in terms of themselves and their art. This is perfectly legitimate, but can lead to them possibly reaching the highest realms artistically, but remaining economically unsuccessful. There are millions of artists in various fields and quite a few of them also create high quality works.[23]

The difference in the market is only partly due to quality. The rest has to do with how much artists can empathize with their buyers and meet their needs - as different as they may be - in terms of investing in art. Of course, it is also true that someone who wants to please everyone may end up being of no real interest to anyone. So it's worth developing a picture for yourself of who the buyer you're targeting is, why they're buying and what they want in order to arrive at a buying decision. This can influence both the way you present yourself, but more importantly, and often more importantly, the way you communicate and interact.

Long-term benefit instead of one-time purchase

One technique that many successful NFT providers have also taken advantage of is to offer existing customers additional deals for a period of time.

Imagine, for example, that you offer existing owners of your NFTs to regularly (for example annually) acquire another NFT offered only to them (for example in a limited edition) either at a special price or possibly even for free. Such an approach could be beneficial for you as a supplier (customer loyalty, community, possibly upselling, Royaltys as a share of the resale of the artwork, even if you gave it away for free) as well as be of interest to the owner of the NFTs (more attractive in resale, additional contact to "his artist", long-term profit and recognition, etc.). Of course, besides free NFTs, other longer-term issues are also conceivable, as Gary Vee, for example, exemplifies with his conferences.

Sometimes the selling price is not the goal

This was already addressed in the previous section. NFTs can also play a role, for example, simply to have additional access and contact with fans. Some providers also use NFTs as membership cards for the fan club or give away NFTs as a thank you for loyal fans. By using Royaltys, money can also be acquired if the community is successful and grows accordingly. Sometimes, however, it makes more sense to think about what you can do for your fans and admirers first than to focus primarily on your own wallet.

Learn and communicate: Use social media

Social media offers an almost infinite variety of different platforms and media, which can be used to learn, bond with customers and prospects, communicate with them (not only in one direction) or even to build entire ecosystems. We will then look at a few examples of platforms and possible areas of use. It goes without saying that while it makes more than sense to be inspired by the examples mentioned, you can also discover, try out and, if successful, retain your own new approaches and uses.

[1] Https://www.christies.com/features/Monumental-collage-by-Beeple-is-first-purely-digital- artwork-NFT-to-come-to-auction-11510-7.aspx

[2] Source: https://niftygateway.com/marketplace/artist/7231

[3] Source: https://niftygateway.com/marketplace/collection/0x12f28e2106ce8fd8464885b80ea865e98b465149/1

[4] Source: https://veefriends.com/

[5] Source: https://veefriends.com/collectibles/accountable-ant

[6] there are also offers on other platforms such as Opensea

[7] https://veefriends.com/friends/3292-forgiving-horned-frog

[8] https://discord.com/invite/veefriends

[9] https://techcrunch.com/2021/05/11/cryptopunks-nft-bundle-goes-for-17-million-in-christies-auction/

[10] Source: https://www.coindesk.com/price/bitcoin/ on 17.2.2022 – 8.30h

[11] https://www.theverge.com/2021/5/11/22430254/cryptopunks-christies-sale-larva-labs

[12] at Christie's

[13] https://www.larvalabs.com/cryptopunks

[14] this pretty much calls into question statements in the press according to which NFTs are already declining in importance again.

[15] Source: https://meebits.larvalabs.com/

[16] Source: https://www.youtube.com/c/KygoMusic

[17] Source for quote and image: https://niftygateway.com/collections/kygoopens

[18] Source: https://boredapeyachtclub.com/

[19] Source: https://onlineonly.christies.com/s/no-time-present/yuga-labs-est-2021-14/129345

[20] Source: https://opensea.io/collection/boredapeyachtclub

[21] Source: https://opensea.io/collection/bored-ape-chemistry-club

[22] Source: https://twitter.com/boredapeyc

[23] whereby I do not want to presume to decide here who belongs to which category

CHAPTER FOUR

NFT Selling – don't leave it to chance

Among the hundreds of social media channels and providers, there are some that are of particular interest in the context of NFT providers. Let's take a closer look at a few of them. In doing so, I am only concerned with positioning here. There are countless other publications, online media and much more on the subject of setting up and building up appropriate presences and channels. In the following, I will therefore focus on a brief positioning of the channels in question and a few examples of possible applications in the context of NFT, and leave it to you to select platforms that are suitable for you and then deal more intensively with their use. Of course, this is only a selection. Depending on the use case, there will undoubtedly be other, additionally interesting sites and apps. For example, Soundcloud might be of interest if you are a music creator, or platforms like 500pc, FotoCommunity or YouPic if you are a photographer.

Instagram

Instagram is used by many artists who present their works there. Not only is it possible to upload images and videos, but also to interact with one's community. This can be done via direct messages, interaction based on comments, but also by creating short video feeds or series of them.

Through the use of videos, music creators also use the channel to showcase their work. The platform has an enormous reach of over 1 billion different users who are active at least once a month, in many cases several times a day. Posts can be categorized through the use of up to 30 #hashtags per post. NFT is a big issue here. The corresponding hashtag #NFT has over 7 million posts, but even compound hashtags like #nftsale still bring it to over 100,000 posts. Examples for the use of the platform: presentation of works (image/video) and creative process (video), interaction with the community, advertising for own NFTs and works with the possibility of linking to corresponding profiles, possibly with the help of further apps like linktree.com and more. Instagram is building its own marketplace. In my opinion, it still needs some time until it is really good. It's certainly worth taking a closer look at it, too, so that you can offer other products there besides NFT, such as prints, sound recordings, or similar things.

Tip: By using a (free) "Business Account" you can additionally use many statistics functions, which allow you to better plan your activities and measures and also to better assess the interaction of your followers or likers.

Facebook

Facebook probably doesn't need to be made particularly known to anyone anymore. Everyone knows the name today and has at least a vague idea of what this platform represents and offers. The platform was founded in 2004 by Mark Zuckerberg and is undoubtedly one of the social media platforms with the widest reach. The Facebook group, now Meta Platforms, also includes other sites and offers such as WhatsApp, Instagram and many others.

Facebook offers the possibility to operate different sites for one person. For example, if you have an existing site that is only for personal friends and family, and you want to keep the posts there more private, you can of course run a parallel but separate site for yourself as an artist, where you interact with customers, prospects, and fans.

Facebook offers not only the possibility for people to follow your posts, but also to build communities of friends and fans with corresponding group and community functions, as well as marketplaces and more. The reach on Facebook is enormous and today is by no means reserved for private individuals. Even a company, whether it is a one-man operation, a sideline business or a large corporation, can hardly manage without a presence(s) on Facebook. In addition, of course, Facebook - like almost all social media sites - also offers the possibility of placing advertisements. This can be quite cost-effective if it is done well and used in a very targeted manner.

TikTok

TikTok has a reputation for attracting mainly teenage users. This was indeed the case for a long time, but it has changed in the meantime and the proportion of adult users, including those of a more mature age, is constantly increasing. This platform also currently appeals to over 100 million people in Europe alone, who use it regularly. Worldwide, the number of users is in the billions. In the course of 2022, it is expected to reach 1.5 billion people. Even if you only address one per thousand of the users here and count them as part of the target group, we are talking about 100,000 people in Europe alone. So it doesn't have to scare anyone off that perhaps 70% of users are unlikely to be potential fans or customers. On the other hand, even teenagers get older over time and may become interested in your art.

Basically, TikTok is not unlike Instagram. The only difference is that instead of focusing on pictures, the focus here is on short videos, which are often designed in such a way that they encourage viewers to interact to a certain extent (dance along, sing along, copy challenges, etc.). Many users report that posts that might get a few dozen likes on Instagram can gain thousands on TikTok if they are designed to be TikTok-compatible.

Undoubtedly, people who use TikTok are somewhat different in preferences and lifestyle than users of some other platforms, but that is always the case anyway. Every platform attracts its own audience, and to be successful on it, you need to understand what makes users tick, what they're looking for on the platform, and how they interact. Artists in the field of music or electronic media may be able to score particularly well here. But you can also find classic photographers who post short tutorials or insights into the creation process here, for example ... Admittedly, these don't appeal to thousands. Some also use TikTok as a second platform, so to speak, in order to reuse videos that they produce for Instagram here (Attention: In this case, certain framework conditions in terms of duration, etc. must be observed).

YouTube

You may also be familiar with the saying that YouTube is no longer just a video portal, but has become one of the largest international search engines. When they have a question or a problem, many people first look on YouTube to see if there are any answers. There you can find even such earth-shattering topics as tutorials on how to peel off Post-its correctly. On the other hand, of course, there are also entries where you don't really know whether the creator simply wanted to make fun of the visitors or whether he really didn't know any better and posted a video proof of his own ignorance.

In fact, the platform, which was founded in 2005 by Paypal employees and sold to Google just one year later, offers a unique way to reach people and gradually build a relationship with them.

For example, an acquaintance did this by taking users on his photo shoots as a photographer (landscapes) and teaching them about his own techniques (image composition, technique) as well as about beautiful photo spots. In addition, he also linked used products via affiliate links in the description. The result was that today he has several tens of thousands of subscribers who interact with him on an ongoing basis: They like, comment, but also order products, from which he also gets a commission through the affiliate links. Then, when he has produced a new video, he publicizes it on his other profile pages such as Instagram, Facebook and Twitter, for example, and thus achieves additional hits and customer loyalty. In addition, he gets orders for shoots, offers photo courses and trips and, of course, sells his own work.

Of course, the same could be done for painters, graphic artists, musicians, etc. The theme is always the same: building community by offering benefits and building relationships. Only too willingly, many of the community members will also purchase products, whether those that are advertised or their own artwork, and also seek further opportunities for interaction.

Creators of videos with larger numbers of users can also benefit from Youtube's advertising revenue, and of course there is also the option of additional paid advertising.

Pinterest

Pinterest is probably a social media site that many people are not really familiar with. Perhaps one or the other has already read the name or seen the site's logo, a red "P" in a white round field surrounded by a red round frame. Comparatively few (compared to the aforementioned platforms) actively use the site, however. The site can be described as a sharing and social media service that allows information to be stored and discovered using images and videos on pinboards.

The platform was founded in 2009 and went live about a year later. It can be assumed that about 2 billion search queries are generated on this platform per month. Most of the users come from the American region. But in Germany, for example, around 4 million items of content are saved every day. It is also interesting to note that around ¾ of access is via mobile access (phone) and over ¼ of users also use the app for purchases. This figure is particularly impressive based on an analysis by Statista:

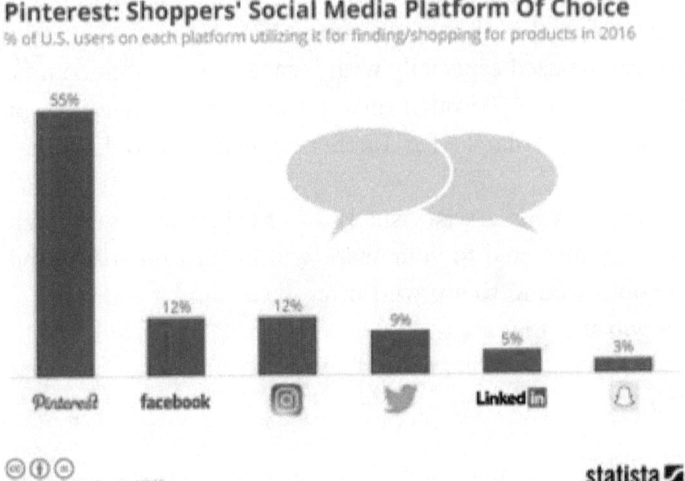

[1]
Some of the buyers purchase corresponding services and products directly on Pinterest's marketplace. Of course, there are also people who study offers on Pinterest and then purchase them elsewhere. The platform is also particularly interesting because it often appeals to people with a higher level of education and better financial means, who are also interested in topics such as culture and lifestyle.

Twitter

Can it be that there's anyone who doesn't know Twitter! Tweets like President Trump's have managed to be talked about in the global media landscape for years. Tweets have helped organize people - for example, during the Arab Spring, when various peoples sought to emancipate themselves from their often questionable governments. But tweets are also used by stars, starlets, and any number of "normal" people to share their activities, sensitivities, opinions, successes, and failures with the world.

An important part of the success is the fact that the platform is not used to distribute huge letters and documents, but to send and exchange short messages.

The platform was founded in 2006 and is now one of the most successful and largest social media platforms. It is free for private use. Incidentally, Twitter derives its name from "to twitter," which means to tweet. This is also where the cute bird in the logo comes from.

Twitter can be used especially with regard to a constant communication with your community. Through retweets and similar measures, the whole thing is also very suitable for further spreading and building a larger community.

Particularly if your art is visually oriented, it may very well be that people who are attracted to your work will in turn retweet it and thereby also get people around them, who often have similar interests, to take an interest in you and your art.

Snapchat

Most people won't think of Snapchat directly when it comes to a social media platform that can be used in business. Many probably first think of an app that young people use to share pictures and videos with each other. In fact, a very important feature of Snapchat is that sent texts, images and videos do not remain as in other platforms and can therefore be viewed again and again or even reused if necessary. In Snapchat, sent posts are only displayed for a short time (the time in seconds can be selected by the sender) and then disappear again.

Snap Inc. was founded in 2011 by three former Stanford students. It owns other services in addition to Snapchat. Today, the messaging app is used by very different user groups. A significant proportion are young people, often in their teens, who use it to communicate with friends.

In addition, the fact that images only appear briefly and then "disappear" - insofar as they are not saved on the recipient's page as a screenshot, for example - is often also used by adult content performers. It can also be seen that more and more companies are discovering the platform as a means of contacting customers.

Basically, we have to ask ourselves with Snapchat whether the platform can actually be useful for our use case. After all, just under 10% of female Snapchat users are over 35 years old, and over 5% of male users. Of these, certainly not all of them fall into the "adult content" category. However, you have to assess for your specific use case whether the corresponding people correspond to your target audience and whether it is worth interacting with them in this way (community building / interaction / offering works).

Reddit

Reddit is a social media aggregator. That is, it is a website where registered users can post content such as links, videos, images, polls, or text posts that are rated by other users.

These ratings influence the position of the entry on the Reddit website. The site has been online since 2005, making it one of the older offerings in the social media sector, and with over 400 million users, it is also one of the larger sites. Statista shows for this platform, for example in Germany (2017), that around 12% of all internet users aged 30-39 and 6% of all internet users aged 40-49 use Reddit.

Reddit is the 6th most visited site in the world. Over ½ billion people visit the site every month. This is undoubtedly a size that makes it worth taking a closer look at this platform.

There are thousands of entries on the topic of NFT, but also entire communities that deal with the topic. The same applies to topics such as art, music and photography, whereby there are of course also numerous specific subgroups for all these areas, in which one can both exchange information and advertise one's own offers. Of course, one can also advertise one's own works here or inform about them and thus in turn address people who are interested in the topic anyway (by correctly classifying corresponding entries).

Flickr, Glass, 500px, youpic, photocommunity

For photographers, the above-mentioned sites and apps can be a way to get in touch with other photographers and photo enthusiasts and get feedback from like-minded people.

However, for the purpose of building a fan and customer community, the sites mentioned do not seem to be very suitable in my experience.

Unless, of course, they find a way or method that I have not yet discovered. Nevertheless, participation can be helpful, on the one hand to increase reach and presence, and on the other hand to potentially find customers. You can find the websites as follows:

- Flickr: https://www.flickr.com/
- Glass: https://glass.photo/
- 500px: https://500px.com/
- youpic: https://youpic.com/
- photocommunity: https://www.fotocommunity.com/

Tumblr

Tumblr is a social media provider that some commentators keep pronouncing dead. In preparing this book, I learned from a wide variety of authors read that this website is long past the zenith of its importance and hardly attractive anymore. But is that really the case? Let's check the numbers: As of the beginning of 2022, the platform counts over ½ billion users who maintain their own blog on Tumblr, i.e. transport their own content via the website. Beepl, for example, who was mentioned earlier, runs his blog on Tumblr continuously and publishes his daily artwork there: https://beeple.tumblr.com/. There are also current statistics which state that about 7.5% of Internet users use Tumblr. That is quite an impressive figure.

In the context of our concern, NFT, it is safe to say that a micro-blogging platform always has a different approach and a different type of interaction than, for example, a platform like Facebook, Twitter or Instagram, where a certain type of direct interaction is possible.

Basically, you can create your own sites in Tumblr and write entries in the following formats:

- Text entries
- Photos
- Quotes
- Links
- Chats
- Audio

- Video

This means that essentially all types of interaction are possible, which we are otherwise also familiar with from social media platforms. What is somewhat special in this platform is the possibility - if desired - to also use your own site with your own domain. So you can not only use a web address like myname.tumblr.com, but also directly myname.com or similar.

However, this then requires that you purchase a corresponding domain. Whether this is useful or sensible in your case, you will undoubtedly have to decide for yourself.

Now, in terms of use in the NFT context, interacting on a site like Tumblr is undoubtedly more geared towards the long term. The site can be used - as used by beepl, for example - to show your development and thus represent a long-term build-up of your work, so to speak, or to exchange with your community and to bind them to you. In the context of direct community building in the sense of community acquisition, I think that forms of interaction that focus on a faster exchange among community members are better suited.

Telegram

You're probably surprised that I'm including Telegram, probably one of the most well-known messenger providers, in this presentation. Don't worry: I'm not going to suggest that they sell their NFTs over the phone. At least not in the way you might have feared.

In fact, Telegram can be used to create groups of up to 200,000 users and also provides tools such as autoresponders and others, which are used by many professional users as a good alternative to costly email marketing approaches. Telegram can also be used without having to have a cell phone turned on or nearby. Clients exist for all common computer platforms such as PC, Mac or Linux in addition to traditional clients for popular cell phones such as Android, iPhone or iPad.

Channels are a central topic in the context of Telegram. The creator can decide whether only he or other people have write access in these channels. This makes it possible to organize both approaches in the sense of pure information distribution as well as those for interaction with a community (and among community members themselves). Whoever joins such a channel will continuously receive new information. They can decide whether they want news to pop up as notifications on their cell phones or whether they want to call them up actively.

Such messages can also be linked to each other (even across channels). Links to the Internet are also possible (e.g., to other social media platforms or to specific offers). To manage your presence, you can also use extensive analytics and interaction automation in the form of easy-to-use bots or simple feedback and comment functions. Such features are possible on other platforms as well, but Telegram stands out for something special: Users here do have to provide a phone number to register, but it is not displayed to other users, which offers the possibility of simpler and more private exchanges with users. You might not want the whole fan community bombarding you with calls 24/7!

In the NFT context, Telegram can be used to operate a very close community with its own users. Not only can information be sent (scheduling options etc. are also available) and responses from community members be edited (also automated with bots).

Telegram can also be used as a communication hub that can be used to link posts and information across a wide variety of websites. It may also be of interest that you can also run multiple channels, some of which get the same content, and some of which get different content. So one possible application could be that you run an open channel that anyone can join and where you provide information about yourself and your works. Additionally you could run a closed channel, which is only available to NFT owners. In this closed group you can provide further information, make exclusive offers to your fans or possibly enable another form of interaction.

WhatsApp

WhatsApp is a social media tool, a messenger that has one of the largest user numbers ever and is actively used by a large number of users many times a day. Whatsapp status alone is used by about 450 million people every day.

This means that incoming messages from users are noticed and possibly even answered within a few seconds or minutes, even in a large number of cases. These key figures also make the platform interesting for marketing business users.

Basically, the same applies to WhatsApp as to Telegram: Here, too, you can communicate with registered participants of a group and send them news and information. You can communicate with groups to which you actively invite people, as well as with groups to which "anyone" who is interested can register. This allows for fine-grained, targeted communication. Chatbots can also be used in Whatsapp. This sounds much more complicated than it actually is.

Basically, the following frequencies have proven successful for communication via messenger (this does not only apply to WhatsApp) depending on the target group for many senders:

- Media (videos, interactions): 3-5 x per day
- Brands and communities: 1-2x per day
- B2B context: every 1-2 days

Please note: Quantity should never take precedence over quality! So it is better to send only one message per day, which then also offers benefits for the recipient, than three, which are actually only SPAM. Try to think less about what you get out of the communication and what you would like to have and achieve, but think from the recipient's point of view: What does he get out of receiving your message? If their answer is: "Nothing", they will very soon unsubscribe from your mailing list. Nobody likes SPAM.

Timing is also particularly important when sending. When does your target group use Whatsapp? In many cases, that is:

- In the morning before work (7-9 AM)
- After work (17-19 h)
- Before bedtime (9 PM)

However, if you have a target group that is active in different time zones or comes from countries where a different daily schedule may be common (e.g. Spain with siesta time), then it may be that you should cover completely different time ranges. It is best to test this.

In addition, there are also studies on what is best received on which days and has the best response rates. But here, too, the findings are of course average values and may look different for certain target groups:

- Monday - News and new ideas

- Thursday - Tips and Know-hows
- Saturday - bargains / concrete offers

From a certain size of the community and interaction, you should also familiarize yourself with the offers and possibilities of Whatsapp Business.

Who is the target group and where is it active?

Now we have talked about a large number of different platforms, but there are hundreds more. Some of them are large and address a wide audience, others are more specialized and focused on a specific group of users and their needs.

Of course, it is neither economical nor sensible or possible to play on all platforms and to be present everywhere. In fact, however, this is not even necessary. Success in this context does not lie in the mass of different platforms that are used, but rather in their selection - which should correspond to the intended target audience - and the quality of the presence there in the form of contributions and interactions.

But how do you find the right platform? To do this, you first need to answer a seemingly simple question: "Who is my target audience?" Until you can answer this question, any further activity will have the success of a shotgun shell fired in black night in any direction. It may well be that something hits - but the probability is not particularly high and the scattering loss is enormous.

Now, yes, one might be tempted to answer the question as follows: "The target audience is anyone who could possibly buy my NFTs or knows someone who might buy one." Many - usually unsuccessful - companies have these kinds of definitions of target audience. If "everyone" is your target audience, how are you going to design targeted actions and communications? Even then, you're stuck with the "shotgun blast system." Consequently, define more narrowly and precisely!

There may well be someone who buys from you once but doesn't fall into your target audience. But you still need as narrow a focus as possible on which they can direct your force. Only then will you not get bogged down. And probably building a social media presence is not your central concern, but you use it only to become additionally present as an artist and to get additional sales channels, including those via NFTs.

Of course, there can also be different groups, which come into question as a target audience. In fact, that is often the case. We have already talked in an earlier section about the fact that people may buy NFTs for very different reasons. These people often represent different target audiences. However, to avoid getting bogged down, I would recommend that you start with a specific target group, and once you have achieved initial results, move on to another target group based on the experience you have gained. You can continue this procedure as long as it is possible within your capacity.

Once you have a clear picture of who your target audience is, you should look at the different platforms to see if your target audience is present there and how the type of interaction takes place. In doing so, you should pay attention to whether the target audience you are addressing is also looking for what you are offering in this context.

It may be, for example, that someone belongs to your target customer area, but does not exchange information about art or investments on a particular platform, but simply uses it, for example, to arrange leisure activities with friends, etc. It is ideal if you can get in touch with people from your target customer area and ask them directly. If you do this not just with one person, where "outliers" are always possible, but survey a representative number, you will find out where an investment of time is most likely to pay off.

In doing so, you should also focus again. Use one or two platforms and, when you achieve initial successes through them, decide whether you need more.

Maybe one or 2 platforms are already enough to get in touch with the target group in the way you envision. It's also always possible that you bet on the wrong horse. If one platform doesn't deliver, you should also be ready to switch.

However, you should be aware that building a presence on a social media platform often takes several quarters. Short-term successes here are more likely to be lucky hits than the rule.

Next, I'd like to show you a way to professionalize the effort of maintaining your social media presence on the one hand, and also make it more efficient on the other.

[1] Source: https://www.statista.com/chart/7025/pinterest_-shoppers-social-media-platform-of-choice/

CHAPTER FIVE

A little additional tip on the subject of working with social media sites

If you use several social media platforms or would like to use them in a more structured way than just occasionally when you have time to make a post, you can use social media management platforms to your advantage, which can control a wide range of social media sites and supply them with posts (also time-controlled). In addition, some of these social media management platforms offer additional functions in connection with the editing of comments or even analysis functions.

Of course, there are differences here. Social media management websites differ considerably in the number of connected platforms, the depth of the corresponding connections, the functions, but also the prices. In any case, it is advisable to get an overview based on your own needs, especially since many of these platforms are also developing very quickly and pricing models are constantly changing for some of them.

I would like to mention two examples at this point, although their mention should not be taken as a recommendation.

Hootsuite

Hootsuite is a social media management platform created in 2008. The system's user interface takes the form of a dashboard and supports social network integration for Twitter, Facebook, Instagram, LinkedIn, Pinterest and YouTube. Other platforms can be integrated and controlled more or less deeply via additional integration functions.

Hootsuite is based in Vancouver and employs nearly 1000 people. The company has more than 18 million users in over 175 countries, most of whom operate multiple accounts on different platforms. Many of the users are not page creators themselves, but media agencies that operate accounts for their clients.

The platform covers all requirements that can be placed on classic social media marketing. In addition to a feature-reduced free version, there are various levels of subscriptions, which differ in terms of the number of social media accounts used and managed, as well as in a variety of additional functions. At the time of writing, subscriptions cost between 39 and 669 euros per month, with an additional Enterprise plan whose price is based on the needs of users (but is probably over 669 euros per month). In any case, it's worth trying out the platform during a free trial, even within its full range of functions, if you see social media more intensively as part of your marketing efforts and operate accounts on multiple platforms.

Heropost

The platform Heropost.io, also based in Canada, has increasingly positioned itself as a low- cost alternative to Hootsuite in recent years. Recently, it has often advertised a lifetime deal for a one-time fee of US$ 197 (without subscription costs). Which of course weighs in against an approach of at least €39 per month with Hootsuite. This can undoubtedly be seen as an approach to poach more established market players. As a user, I got the impression that the functions are good, but not yet on the same level as Hootsuite.

Nevertheless, the platform can be an interesting alternative, especially in the beginning and for people who do not want to invest a lot of money.

As I said, those were just two providers. There are quite a few more. In any case, it's worth taking a closer look at these and similar tools if you understand social media as an important part of your market strategy.

CHAPTER SIX

Frequently asked questions

A new market and a new model for generating income always mean a certain degree of uncertainty. To this end, let me address a few of the questions most frequently raised in this context and answer them as far as possible:

The NFT and cryptocurrency markets seem to be slipping lately. Does investing and participating in the market make sense at all?

In fact, in "uncertain times" people tend to invest their money in a way that allows them to access it quickly when needed. As a result, in such times, corresponding investments tend to rise in value, while forms of investment that can be used less quickly tend to fall in value. As a result, demand for gold and hard currencies usually rises, the value of equities tends to fall somewhat, and demand for investment forms such as art and the like declines significantly. At the same time, however, there are also investors who actively use precisely such slumps in prices and demand to acquire good, long-term investments at favorable prices.

Overall, it is safe to say that the demand for NFTs tends to weaken due to uncertainties in the world. However, if we assume that such uncertainties and crises will also pass again, one can also use these uncertainties with regard to one's own work to build up a foothold in this market right now and to already be present and known at the next upswing. Last but not least, quite a few works from the NFT sector have already been sold or auctioned off for millions in the current year.

Where are the risks?

Like any procedure that can bring success and profit, working with NFTs also involves risks. However, if we disregard the general risks on the Internet, there are also risks in the context of NFTs themselves. The most frequently encountered and reported problem lies in the costs incurred by the creation and handling of NFT (gas fees). Depending on the platform and cryptocurrency / blockchain, these can vary greatly and in many cases this happens with every transaction on the blockchain. These include:

ax.   Buying and selling cryptocurrencies
ax.   Exchange of cryptocurrencies among themselves
ax.   Create, buy and sell NFTs, etc.

In addition, there are often commissions from platform operators and the like.

Such transaction costs can be in the cent range, but especially in the context of Ethereum they are sometimes in the three-digit euro range. However, there is hope that Ethereum version 2.0 will be released in the summer of 2022, which will significantly reduce energy consumption and costs through a different transaction procedure. In other blockchains, the corresponding costs are often actually negligible.

In any case, it is advisable to carefully examine all costs incurred before creating and offering NFTs. With the right decisions, significant revenues are possible. In extreme cases, the wrong decisions can lead to transaction costs that are several times higher than the sales proceeds. Since costs, gas fees and conditions can also change continuously, no particular course of action can be recommended here.

How secure are my NFTs and how secure are cryptocurrencies?

Recently, we have been reading more and more press reports about NFTs or cryptocurrency being stolen, for example. Both are actually only possible if the owners disregard security precautions on their part. In most cases, it is a matter of owners not keeping their passwords or other access data secure. Either they were stored on a PC, which was then hacked, or they were voluntarily given out because they fell for a phishing attempt. As long as you keep your password safe, make sure you only enter it on sites and apps that are real and trustworthy (not some bogus portals or the like), and above all, don't give it to third parties (neither friends, family, nor any people who claim to be from a sales platform or the police, for example), the risk should be fairly manageable. Regarding the latter, a professional platform will never ask you to send your passwords or other credentials to it. It has no need for that, since it has access to everything it needs for its administrative tasks via administration rights. Anything else is not their job.

Accordingly, it does not need any passwords or information.

Is the whole thing even legal?

As long as you abide by the laws of your country, such as tax law, and do not use the acquired income for unlawful things, there is no reason, at least currently, why the aforementioned procedures should be illegal.

In fact, due to the fact that cryptocurrencies in particular are sometimes also used by criminals, certain reservations exist in some countries, so that regulations are also being sought within the framework of legal initiatives. However, to my knowledge, this is currently not the case in any Western country in a way that would make the use of NFTs or cryptocurrencies illegal. However, it is of course always a good idea to verify the current state of legislation in one's own country and, of course, to adhere to it.

Afterword

Bratee, Dirtea and Haftea are just three examples of how various rappers use their fame to open up further markets and sources of income in completely different areas - in this case as "inventors" of iced teas. As romantic as the idea of an artist who devotes his entire life to his art and does nothing else may be, in most cases he will tend to live in poverty. This is not a valuation of his art. However, we already know from history the image of the poor artist who looked for a rich patron - in earlier times often coming from the high nobility - and was virtually there to "decorate" him with his art. In addition, there are many examples of poor and impoverished artists who "did not want to sell" or could not sell and thus lived virtually from hand to mouth.

I think everyone has to decide for himself how he wants to deal with his art and his life. My goal with this work was to give artists of different fields and arts some ideas on how to be successful with their art in the NFT context. On the one hand, I was concerned with the presentation of NFTs and the technical information to understand them; on the other hand, I found it crucial to also address aspects related to marketing and building sustainable success. Only those who also understand these topics and deal intensively with their customers and the corresponding market will also be sustainably successful with a product.

I hope that I have been able to give you many new, interesting ideas. But now comes the most important idea: Success will only come if you become active now at the latest. Just from the fact that you now know what an NFT is, you haven't sold one yet and you don't have one more Euro in your account. So I challenge you: If the NFT market is interesting for you, then start NOW. Put the book aside, start your PC and get active. Even that does not guarantee success. However, there is one approach which is guaranteed not to bring success: doing nothing.

With this in mind, good luck with your new NFT project!

The author

9 798888 157602